FOREWORD
Jennifer, Lady Gretton
President of LOROS

I am delighted to have this opportunity to ⟨…⟩ to this history of LOROS. In 2009 and 201⟨…⟩ f care at Manor Croft, our Day T⟨…⟩ ⟨…⟩. As you will read, these 25 years ⟨…⟩ nd it was decided that the histor⟨…⟩ ⟨…⟩nd how it has developed should ⟨…⟩. The 25th anniversary is a very suitable ti⟨…⟩

I feel very honoured to be Preside⟨nt⟩ of LOROS and to have had the opportunity to see the wonderful work that is and has been done by so many people. My grateful thanks go to them all. Firstly of course to those who had the vision of a hospice in Leicester so many years ago and who had the dedication, determination and foresight to fight for their vision and make it happen. To all the medical staff, past and present, who have devoted themselves to providing that very special care and help to our patients and have helped LOROS develop into the very special organisation it is today. To all the non-medical staff, who do so much to keep the organisation running in so many different but important ways. And finally to all the volunteers, many of whom have been with us since the very beginning, and are so important to the organisation.

My final thanks obviously go to Caroline Wessel who has given up so much of her time to research and write this history. She has produced a meticulous history of LOROS, which charts the progress and development of this very special organisation, which has given and will continue to give so much to the terminally ill of Leicester, Leicestershire and Rutland.

Jennifer, Lady Gretton

Cover illustration: *LOROS staff at the Hospice*

CONTENTS

		page
Foreword	Jennifer, Lady Gretton, President	1
Contents		3
Chapter One	Early Beginnings	5
Chapter Two	Buildings	11
Chapter Three	In-Patient Care	23
Chapter Four	Spiritual, Emotional and Therapeutic Care	35
Chapter Five	Care in the Community	47
Chapter Six	Education and Research	53
Chapter Seven	Volunteers	57
Chapter Eight	Fundraising	67
Chapter Nine	Royal and VIP Visits – a picture gallery	77
Conclusion	Aspirations for the Future, LOROS Trustees	83
Appendix (i)	Time Line of LOROS history	87
Appendix (ii)	Officers, Patrons and Ambassadors	88
Appendix (iii)	Biographies	90
Appendix (iv)	LOROS Services and Aims	93
Bibliography and Acknowledgements		94

Published in United Kingdom in 2012 by LOROS

Copyright © 2011 C.M.Wessel

ISBN 978-0-9572191-0-6

Typeset by
Words & Graphics Limited, Anstey, Leicestershire LE7 7AF

Printed in Great Britain by
Butler Tanner & Dennis, Caxton Road, Frome, Somerset BA11 1NF

CHAPTER ONE
EARLY BEGINNINGS

This account of the Leicestershire & Rutland Organisation for the Relief of Suffering (LOROS) celebrates the first twenty-five years of its remarkable work since 2nd September 1985, the day that the first Hospice patient was admitted. But in fact the idea of providing hospice care in Leicestershire had already been suggested over ten years earlier. On 17th April 1972 a public meeting at Leicester Royal Infirmary, organised by a local charity administrator and a social worker, had recognised the need for a special type of care for the terminally ill. Meanwhile, the Leicester Free Church Women's Council (LFCWC), who ran a residential home for elderly ladies in De Montfort Street, Leicester, had found that there was no decent local provision for their residents who became terminally ill. So the LFCWC invited the Leicester Council of Churches (LCC) to attend a joint meeting with them at Clarendon Park Congregational Church, London Road – and on 12th December 1975, with only seven people present, an idea was conceived that culminated in the birth of LOROS.

The year of 1976 saw some significant developments in the LOROS story. In order to persuade the authorities, trusts and individuals of the urgent need to provide this type of specialised care in Leicestershire, a scientific assessment was carried out, which concluded that terminal illness care was both desirable and effective. At a Project Meeting in July the name of 'Leicester (not Leicestershire; it changed to this in 1984) Organisation for the Relief of Suffering' (LOROS) was formulated. It was decided that LOROS would be non-denominational and would engage with people of any religious or philosophical convictions. At this same meeting a Steering Committee was set up, comprising Dr Andrew Cull (Chairman), Mr Eric Jones (Secretary), Mr Philip Hall (Treasurer), Dr Tony Carr, Mrs Christine Wood and Mr Michael Marvell. In due course Cull, Carr and Marvell became affectionately known as the 'terrible trio', so firm was their resolve to develop the project with urgency. The Steering Committee was tasked with the setting up of a Constitution, and Mr Marvell offered the team some office space at the Friar Lane premises of the charity he administered, Leicester Charity Organisation Society (LCOS).

Between February and June of the following year, the energetic Steering Committee had drawn up the official Constitution; had registered LOROS as a Company Limited by Guarantee; secured it as Registered Charity no. 506120; and organised its affiliation to the Leicester Council of Voluntary Services. A Council of Management was formed, requiring no less than five and no more than fifteen members, who set about working with the Leicestershire Area Health Authority (LAHA) and The National Society for Cancer Relief (NSCR). LOROS's first Public Meeting in November 1977 was attended by over two hundred people, who were enthralled by a lecture given by the well-known Hospice advocate, Dame Cicely Saunders, of St Christopher's Hospice, Sydenham, who spoke on 'The Need for a Continuing Care Service'. Recognition of her principles was to manifest itself in her well-chosen term 'Continuing Care', which now became used instead of the words 'terminally ill'.

Lord Mayor, Cllr Michael Cufflin, and President Lady Palmer with the Hospice plans & models

In 1978 Drs Cull and Carr produced a Paper stating the aims of LOROS. They were:-
- To promote the reduction of distress experienced by the terminally ill and their families
- To offer the highest professional and human standards of care
- To create a team of professionals and volunteers with the necessary skills and human qualities
- To create a domiciliary [home] service for patients
- To admit patients on a short-term basis, until a suitable regime had been established, enabling them to return home in a more comfortable state, both mentally and physically

With regard to finance, it was resolved that a capital sum of £500,000 be raised by public appeal, and that the LAHA should be asked to donate 80% revenue for running costs. In February 1978 the Organisation's first newsletter was published and a register of possible volunteers drawn up. At this time LOROS meetings frequently went on until midnight or later. Often they continued on the pavement outside afterwards. Members arrived home on occasions emotionally exhausted, sometimes wondering if it was all worthwhile. Members might be contacted by telephone at all hours by Dr Cull, who spurred them onwards and expected the same dedication from them as he himself always gave. For many it was a time of tremendous hard work, not always with any apparent progress. Reward came when, at a meeting in May 1979, the LAHA agreed to give financial support to the hospice project, and afterwards the exhilarated LOROS members retired to the home of Dr Carr and drank the champagne he had long previously obtained in anticipation of such a happy outcome from the LAHA.

The years 1980-1983 became a roller-coaster of events. The LOROS logo was designed on discarded cigarette packets and beer mats in the pub. Its black and white circles signified an eclipse and suggested movement either way – from light into darkness, or darkness into light (this logo was replaced by the present one in 1991). A Fundraising Group was started, and a Flower Fund encouraged donations in lieu of funeral flowers. The Bishop of

Leicester, The Rt. Reverend Richard Rutt, consented to become the first LOROS President and the first Administrator, Mrs Anne Kind, was recruited. The Official LOROS Appeal was launched on 2nd March 1981, with its own smart publicity brochure. Fundraising began in earnest and a Publicity Sub-Committee was created. By 1983 the project was expanding so rapidly that the office, 'a small cupboard' at LCOS's Friar Lane offices was outgrown, so in May it moved to 11 Welford Road, Leicester.

In June the ever-swelling LOROS campaign benefitted greatly by a resolution passed in London by the National Federation of Women's Institutes, whose members were "urged to promote and support the provision of hospice care." Leicestershire W.I. groups responded magnificently by providing a deep freeze for the day when the LOROS Day Centre would open, and in due course W.I. branches took it in turn to bake cakes and other goodies to keep the freezer constantly stocked.

In December 1983 another wonderful milestone was reached, when the target of £500,000 was realised. To celebrate, a party was held at the LOROS office, with famous singer and local man, Engelbert Humperdinck, cutting the celebratory cake.

Englebert Humperdinck with wife, Pat, and Lady Palmer, celebrating the reaching of the £ 1/2 million target

The years 1983 and 1984 also saw the start of two other major LOROS projects; the purchase, conversion and opening of Manor Croft, a large Victorian house in Stoneygate, Leicester, as a patients' Day Unit; and the setting up of a Counselling Service for patients and families, run initially from Manor Croft. More information on Manor Croft is given in Chapters 2 and 5, and on Counselling Services in Chapter 4. In 1984 a LOROS Phase II Appeal to Industry was launched, and Lady Palmer, the new President, became Chairman of a Special Appeals Committee, that was to run many successful large-scale fundraising events. And to spread the LOROS message more widely, a Panel of Speakers was formed that toured the county.

By now the building of the new Hospice on the Groby Road site was progressing with speed, and a detailed account of this appears in Chapter 2. With the opening of the LOROS Hospice in 1985, a Thanksgiving Service in Leicester Cathedral, attended by hundreds of supporters and dignitaries, brought to a close the first chapter of the story of the Leicester Organisation for the Relief of Suffering, and set it firmly upon its future course of distinction.

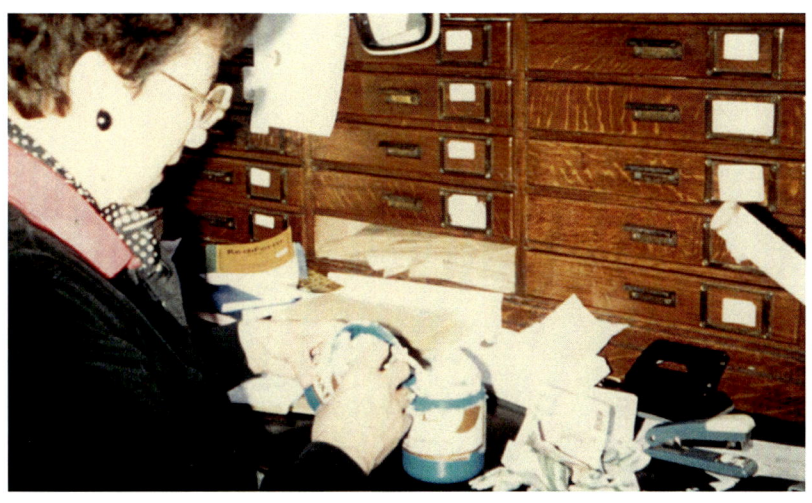

Anne Kind OBE opening a collection box in the Appeals Office, Friar Lane

CHAPTER TWO
BUILDINGS

The LOROS buildings have all been lovingly created or skillfully adapted to suit the specific needs of the Organisation. In 2011 they consist of the Groby Road Hospice complex; the Manor Croft Day Therapy Unit, 147 Ratcliffe Road, Stoneygate; twenty-one LOROS shops spread throughout the area; and a shops warehouse and LOROS Lottery office at 1 Station Road, Glenfield. The Hospice and Manor Croft are owned by LOROS and all the shops and the Station Road premises are leased.

LOROS President, Lady Palmer, cuts the first piece of turf for the new building, 27th March 1984

The LOROS Appeals Office started life as the guest of Leicester Charity Organisation Society at their 18 Friar Lane offices (1976). LOROS Appeals then went to 11 Welford Road (1983), later transferred to 18 De Montfort Street (1995), and, when space became available, finally moved to the Hospice (2001).

The Shops Office started out at the Hospice, and then resided 'over the shop' at the 23 Queens Road store (1992). Later it moved to 29 Kenilworth Drive, an industrial estate unit in Oadby (1995), and from there to the Glenfield shops warehouse (2003), where it remains today

The Hospice
During 1980 a site for the erection of a LOROS Hospice was vigorously considered. Drs Cull, Carr and Kind were amongst those who investigated various options, including Blaby Hall, a unit at Leicester General Hospital, and sites at Thurnby, Scraptoft, Shady Lane in Evington, and Springfield Road, London Road and Carisbrooke Road in Leicester. But a preferred option was to be near the facilities of a general hospital. So when in August 1980 a potential site was offered at the rear of Groby Road Hospital, LOROS accepted it four months later. In May 1982 bore holes were dug on the Groby Road site, preparations for the Hospice building were formulated, and with great excitement a bottle of champagne was cracked open. However in June 1983 a change of location had to be considered, due to the transfer of many departments of Groby Road Hospital to the new Glenfield Hospital. But it was calculated that a move elsewhere would cost LOROS an additional £80,000 and a delay of two years. So at a meeting on August 1983 a decision was made to continue with plans for the Groby Road site.

In January 1984 tenders for the erection of the Hospice were received and John Laing (Construction) Limited were duly appointed as building contractors. The architect was Mr C. Cannell of the Trent Regional Health Authority, with Mr Derek Knightley as Hon. Architect, and Mr John Kelly as Project Manager. On 27th March 1984 LOROS President Lady Palmer officially cut the first piece of 'turf' in preparation for labour to commence, and from then on the work progressed rapidly during the summer months.

People bought bricks for the building at a cost of £1 each, and an Open Day was held for the general public to view progress.

On 31st October 1984 the 'Topping Out' ceremony to celebrate the completion of the structure was performed by the Lord Mayor, Councillor Michael Cufflin, who had raised £115,000 for the LOROS project during his mayoral year. Following the ceremony, a traditional pint of ale was drunk with the workforce and someone placed a sprig of Leylandii over the chapel to 'ward off evil spirits'. According to custom, it should have been a sprig of Yew, but none could be found! Planning for the commissioning of the Hospice then began in earnest. Policies and steering committees were put in place, and a Furnishing Committee planned the colour schemes, furniture, carpets and curtains for the new building.

On three Open Days in April 1985 guided tours of the newly completed Hospice were given. And on 14th June 1985 the builders officially handed over the Hospice to LOROS. Dr Cull received the keys and with great ceremony and excitement opened the front

Lord Mayor, Cllr Michael Cufflin, performs the 'Topping Out' ceremony 1984

door. The first patient was admitted on 2nd September 1985 – and a tremendous milestone had been reached. On 24th February 1986 a full licence was granted to the Hospice to open twenty-five beds (although initially only twelve were used). The single-storey building, surrounding a central courtyard garden, had four bays each with five or six beds, and the remaining beds were in single wards. In addition, there was a reception area, lounge, chapel, kitchens, aviary and a mortuary with viewing room. The original Hospice 'shop' was just a trolley. The Hospice project had cost just under £1,000,000 to build and equip, and another considerable milestone was reached in March 1986 when the total target of £1,500,000 was achieved.

The Hospice was officially opened on 30th May 1986 by Charles and Diana, the Prince and Princess of Wales. Arriving by helicopter, the Prince and Princess were received by local dignitaries and the Princess was presented with a bouquet by one of the nurses, chosen by drawing names out of a hat. The royal couple mingled with

Dr Cull officially receives the keys of the new Hospice from the builders, 14th June 1985

volunteers in a specially erected marquee. They then undertook a tour of the Hospice, and in the chapel heard local schoolchildren singing a specially composed LOROS song. In the ward many members of staff were introduced and the royal couple showed a great interest in their work. It was noticed that the Princess several times sat on patients' beds, talked compassionately with them, and held the hands of some extremely poorly people. After luncheon came the unveiling of a commemorative plaque and the presentation of gifts, after which the Prince and Princess signed an official photograph – though because the Prince's pen would not work the photo had to be sent to Buckingham Palace for his signature! After a 'walk about' amongst the crowds outside, the royal couple departed, and thus ended a memorable and proud day for LOROS.

With the celebrations of the Hospice's 10th Anniversary Year, sufficient money was raised to provide improved overnight stay

The Prince and Princess of Wales sign their official photograph

amenities for a patient's family. The new Relatives' Suite, providing *en suite* facilities for one double and two single visitors' rooms, plus a lounge with TV and hot drink facilities, cost £160,000, and was officially opened by Leicester M.P. Keith Vaz. It continues today to give privacy and dignity to families waiting and grieving together, enabling them to be part of a death, and never making them feel that they should not be there.

After almost fifteen years of hospice care to the people of Leicestershire and Rutland, it was found that the original Hospice building was bursting at the seams. Due to the continual introduction of significant new services for patients and families, more space was urgently needed. Several services were having to share rooms and the Home Care Team was operating from a Portakabin in the Hospice grounds. So in 1999 an appeal for £1,600,000 was launched to fund the building of an imaginative new extension. The architect was Mike Pole and the builders were J.H. Hallam (Contracts) Limited. Additional facilities were to include a new four-bed Day Case Ward for those requiring specialised treatment, and more spacious accommodation for other services, including

Matron Bronwen Biswas helps explain the new facilities to Keith Vaz MP watched by Janet Atkins, Michael Archer and Himat Tana

Lymphoedema and Outpatients Clinics, Counselling, Home Care and Home Sitting Services, Occupational Therapy, Physiotherapy, and complementary therapies such as Aromatherapy, Reflexology and Acupuncture. And, in recognition of the increasing value of LOROS's educational role, two large seminar rooms were planned. Here training could be given not only to LOROS staff, but also to hospital doctors, GPs, nurses and medical students, thus ensuring that the quality hospice care developed by LOROS could be spread and adopted into other settings further afield.

The final cost of the project was £1,800,000. The National Lotteries Charity Board made a grant of £300,000, but the people of Leicestershire and Rutland raised all the rest, save the last £25,000. The LOROS extension was formally opened by the Duchess of Gloucester on 11th May 2000, when she expressed delight at meeting so many patients, staff, trustees and volunteers, whom she felt made the Hospice a very special place. The Duchess was taken on a tour of the new building, and graciously unveiled a commemorative plaque. A happy postscript to this story is that Hallam, the builders, won a coveted Merit Award for Craftmanship for the LOROS extension – maintaining the model of excellence that surrounds the LOROS image.

Completion of the roof of Willow Wing in 2009

In addition to the new extension, the Hospice gardens were given a remarkable makeover. 75 new trees and 3,800 shrubs were planted, and two new courtyards created with a peaceful bamboo area, two pools, and a new purpose-built aviary. The public were invited to sponsor trees, shrubs, garden seats, fish, birds or pool plants and they gave enthusiastically.

In 2003 interior alterations to the Hospice were undertaken, bringing the number of in-patient beds up to thirty-one. Four new single rooms, each with piped oxygen, wall mounted televisions and *en suite* facilities, were created in the 'back corridor', and the five- and six-bedded bays were reduced to four beds. This gave patients with more complex needs greater privacy, and a better space for interventionist treatment. Alterations also included a new family room with double bed option, enabling partners to remain with patients whilst at the Hospice.

Plans for a further large-scale Hospice extension to provide more single room accommodation commenced in 2007. The aim was to provide eleven new single patient rooms, with patios and garden views, increasing the total to nineteen singles, instead of the former eight. This would create over 4,000 additional bed days per year in single rooms, although the bed number would remain at thirty-one. A Public Appeal for £2 million was launched and potential benefactors were

Duchess of Gloucester tours the LOROS extension in 2010

presented with a variety of 'naming' opportunities, ranging from the considerable expense of a room to £350 for a named paving stone. On March 17th 2010, in the Hospice's 25th Anniversary Year, the Duchess of Gloucester returned to officially open the new Willow Wing. She viewed the new extension, unveiled a plaque and talked with staff and patients, as well as meeting two LOROS patrons, snooker star, Mark Selby and Leicester City legend Alan Birchenall. The nursing staff chose the name of Willow Wing because of the fine willow tree that had to be removed for the new building, and the willow tree bower that graces the central garden, under which some patients have wished to spend their last moments in the tranquility of nature.

Creating the right environment is essential. Patients and families have said after admission to the LOROS Hospice – "we now feel safe."

Manor Croft

The suggestion of a Day Unit for terminally ill patients was first mooted in 1983 and a Day Unit Steering Committee, chaired by Mrs Barbara Keene, was set up to seek out suitable properties in the city. The Committee eventually discovered a large Victorian house, previously a family home and then a University Hall of Residence, called Manor Croft at 147 Ratcliffe Road, Leicester. It is a light airy

Duchess of Kent with staff and patients at Manor Croft

house with high ceilings in a pleasant leafy area on the outskirts of Leicester with peaceful gardens. Manor Croft was considered suitable for conversion to a Day Centre, so was purchased in the autumn of 1983 for £84,000. Building alterations commenced almost immediately, with Mr Michael Fergusson as architect, and the final cost including alterations was £107,000. Manor Croft first opened its doors in April 1984.

An imaginative extension at Manor Croft was completed in Spring 1990, increasing potential patient numbers from fifteen to twenty-five. An attractive new large lounge was built, with a verandah and views of the beautiful garden. The old lounge was converted into a Smoking Room and Hairdressing and Beauty Salon for men and ladies. A peaceful Rest Room caters for those feeling a little unwell, and a second outside entrance with ramp assists those in wheel-chairs. An unusual architectural feature was the replacement of drain pipes with chains that take water from the guttering to the ground. On a sunny 25th July 1990 the beautiful Duchess of Kent performed the Official Opening of the extension and radiated warmth and care to every patient. To enable all eighty of them to meet her, a marquee was erected on the car park, where the Duchess took afternoon tea and talked and joked with everyone.

LOROS Shops
When Michael Archer arrived as General Manager at LOROS in 1989 he brought with him considerable retailing expertise. It was therefore decided to experiment with the opening of a LOROS charity shop. It was a most successful venture, and from then onwards new shops have been opened almost every year. Those operating in 2011 are listed below:-

Loughborough, 1A Wards End, (August 1989 – closed Feb 2006)
Hinckley (March 1990)
Birstall (June 1990)
Oadby (July 1990)
Market Harborough (Sept 1990)
Anstey (December 1990)
Oakham (November 1991)
Leicester, Queen's Rd (May 1992)

Leicester, Uppingham Rd (Sept 1994)
Syston (Spring 1995)
Wigston (Spring 1998)
Coalville (Spring 1998)
Leicester, Uppingham Rd, furniture shop (Aug 1998)
Leicester, Queen's Rd, book shop (Sept 1999)
Melton Mowbray (Spring 2000)
Loughborough, Biggin St (Sept 2000)
Blaby (April 2007)
Leicester, Narborough Rd (Spring 2008)
Leicester, Market Place (January 2010)
Loughborough, Devonshire Sq (Feb 2010)
Glenfield, Station Rd, shop + warehouse (2010)

CHAPTER THREE
IN-PATIENT CARE

"What a wonderful change in my life since I have belonged to LOROS", remarked an appreciative patient. The main aim of hospice care is to improve the quality of life for end-of-life patients, helping them to live their lives in the fullest possible way. Care of the whole patient and their families is provided by a multi-disciplinary team. The recognition of each patient's individuality and choice is of enormous importance, and all care is patient centred. The patient, once stabilised, may be able to return home, before dying either at home or in the hospice. But nothing happens to the patient. . . without the patient.

At the time that the LOROS Hospice opened, there were three elements regarding end-of-life care that were still in their infancy, but which were to completely revolutionise the way that final illness came to be managed. Firstly, the very concept of hospice care was only just developing into a speciality. It had been spearheaded by Dame Cicely Saunders at St Christopher's Hospice, Sydenham, London, which opened in 1966. Secondly, the new practice of Counselling was assisting people to understand and deal with

Chairman Barbara Keene, Dr Sam Ahmedzai with his wife, and Dr Edna Clitheroe

their emotions, their anxieties and their relationships. And, lastly, techniques in pain and symptom relief were vastly improving, so that patients realised pain could be effectively controlled by appropriate treatment, making them more comfortable, less apprehensive, and as a result keen to enjoy the last period of their lives to the full.

When Leicestershire's own Hospice first opened in 1985 it was a very simple affair, focussing mainly on medical care, with only twelve beds in use. The first Management Team was small – but was both inspired and inspirational. Robert Alderton was Bursar; Bronwen Biswas was Matron; and Dr Sam Ahmedzai was full-time Medical Director (see Appx iii). After a year another Consultant came part-time, so that Dr Sam could take a holiday. Also appointed were three Nursing Sisters – Lucy Stewart, Wendy Taylor (still a Ward Sister in 2011) and Jean Riley, the first two having been previously at St Christopher's Hospice. There were twenty-nine SRN or SEN qualified nurses in total, and a Steward for after-death care. The LOROS Counselling Service, already operating from Manor Croft, offered sessions at the newly-opened Hospice, where there was also a part-time Chaplaincy Team with Anglican, Roman Catholic and Free Church clergy support. From the outset there was a Hospice Social Worker, providing practical support for patients and families. Within the first year a part-time Physiotherapist and an Occupational Therapist joined the multi-disciplinary Hospice team, and a few years later hairdressing and complementary therapies were added to the services.

Matron Bronwen Biswas recalls the early days – "Nurses were giving all the nursing care, and whilst doing so were able to listen, talk, and communicate, growing to understand all the small nuances of feeling being experienced by the patient. There were three nursing teams, each team covering all shifts, and with its own group of patients, thus ensuring continuity and consistency for patients and families. Despite initial reservations, the volunteer nurses did a marvellous job, and the Team were all of equal importance, including the doctors. In the mid-1980s GPs and District Nurses did not have the specialist skills in pain control to enable a seriously ill patient to remain at home; so LOROS set about providing training for them, in order that patients could stay longer in their homes. After the death of a patient, the whole team would gather together and ask 'Did we do a good job?' and would pinpoint what they had achieved and what could be learned from that experience."

Matron Bronwen continues, "during the first five years of the Hospice, three other elements developed – an Outpatients Clinic in a room on the back corridor; Home Care, whereby nurses went out into patients' homes; and student placements. Third-year student nurses assisted on the ward, and medical students acted as House Officers, thus giving students valuable experience and the Hospice substantial financial benefit."

Some of the staff celebrate the Prince and Princess of Wales's visit in 1986

A second full-time doctor, Dr Ian Johnson, was appointed to the Hospice in 1987. Starting out as its Deputy Medical Director, he became a Consultant in 1990, working alongside Dr Sam Ahmedzai. That same year, a part-time LOROS Consultant Anaesthetist reported on the considerable advances in pain-relief, that greatly improved a patient's comfort. She also succinctly summed up the Hospice experience – "It has been fascinating to watch LOROS grow, both in numbers of staff and experience. In contrast to the hospital hierarchical system, the Hospice has a multi-disciplinary team consisting of doctors from different specialist backgrounds, nurses, dieticians, physiotherapists, occupational and art therapists, social workers and counsellors. We all learn from each other and work together on every aspect of the patients' well being."

Dr Ahmedzai departed in 1994. The following year a new arrival was Consultant, Dr Nicky Rudd, who had previously worked in London as Macmillan Senior Registrar in Palliative Medicine. Dr Rudd set about moving beyond the walls of LOROS, and building up Palliative Care Services in all three University Hospitals of Leicester (UHL). In 1996 when Dr Johnson left LOROS, he summarised its work as "teamwork aimed at getting the best possible quality of life for our patients." In 2006 Dr Luke Feathers became the full-time Lead Consultant, and in 2011 he represents a team that includes four other part-time Consultants, each with their own speciality, who also work within the three UHLs or the community. Dr Feathers carries out administrative, clinical and teaching work, aims to optimise the care of patients with Motor Neurone Disease, and also sits on the End-of-Life Board for Leicestershire. In 2011 the LOROS Hospice has about 700 ward admissions a year, 50%-60% of whom are discharged, and Dr Luke explains that "twenty-five years ago the Hospice gave general palliative care to patients who were right at the end of their life. But now the aim is to plan end-of-life care much earlier on, in conjunction with GPs. Discussions may take place about the future; about where someone would like to die; and the things they would like to do before that happens. The aim is for individualised care."

In 2001, after sixteen years of dedication and vision, Matron Bronwen retired from LOROS, and Chris Faulkner was appointed in her place. Leicestershire-born Chris trained and worked in London and Norwich, then on returning to her home county worked at all three UHLs. At Leicester General Hospital she became a Macmillan Nurse, and on arriving at LOROS declared "I feel passionate about palliative care and being able to develop services here at LOROS, providing a really high standard of care, and developing expertise and knowledge amongst staff. LOROS never stands still, but continually looks at ways of improving." Matron Chris retired in May 2011 and Joanne (Jo) Kavanagh was appointed Director of Care Services in her place. A Registered Nurse and Midwife, Jo has university degrees in various aspects of Health and Management, has held senior appointments in Cancer Services, and was latterly Nurse Director for the East Midlands Cancer Network.

Matron Chris and Matron Bronwen at the 25th anniversary Founders Party

In recent years, Dr Rudd has worked at curtailing the waiting list for LOROS beds by finding other suitable alternatives in hospital or home, so that the Hospice now mainly has cases that cannot be managed elsewhere. These days there is a much greater variety of drugs for pain control, a skill in which LOROS has developed considerable expertise. However the central elements of ward care remain the same as those of the early years described by Matron Bronwen, with a similar system of three nursing teams administering professional but thoughtful and sensitive patient-centred care. As one patient confided, "I'll never forget that we haven't got all the time in the world, and I'll never forget the time other people in the world had for us."

There has been an Enablement Team (formerly called Therapy Team) in place almost from the start of the LOROS story. It works closely with doctors, nurses, family, community and voluntary agencies as well as the LOROS Community Nurse Specialists (CNS), Outpatients Clinic and Manor Croft. The wishes and choices of the patient and family are at the centre of all the Team's work. The Occupational Therapist's aim is to maintain a patient's independence, enabling them to return to their home environment for as long as possible. O.T.s make assessments and can provide equipment such as commodes, chair raisers, and adaptations to the home. The Physiotherapist maximises the patient's mobility

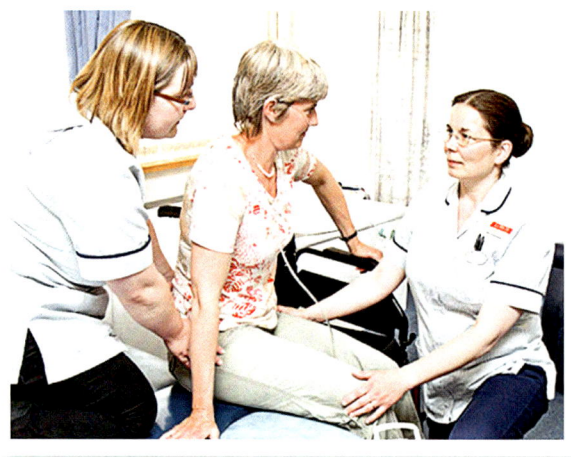

Enablement Team

throughout their illness, so they can remain walking independently for as long as possible. Treatment may include exercise therapy, teaching movement techniques, or the provision of an appropriate walking aid.

The Social Worker supports the discharge process by listening to the wishes of the patient and carer, assesses their needs, and discusses concerns about discharge from the Hospice. And in recent years the Hospice Social Worker also fulfills the ever-increasing need for help with benefits and form-filling, and deals with the new legislation to protect vulnerable adults. Alongside the Social Worker is the Discharge and Liaison (D&L) Team, who support the ward staff to make sure that patients who go home have the appropriate professional care in place. The D&L Team ensures that patients have information and services to allow them to make informed decisions and choices about where they wish to be cared for. They can provide information to assist with future care, and can also commission outside services such as District Nurses, Home Care Agencies and Mobile Meals Service.

A further aid to relieve suffering is the LOROS Lymphoedema Clinic. Set up in 1966, it treats both malignant and non-malignant cases. Lymphoedema is a chronic swelling, usually to the legs or arms, and can occur following cancer treatment. Limbs swell up to often twice or three times the normal size, causing great discomfort and

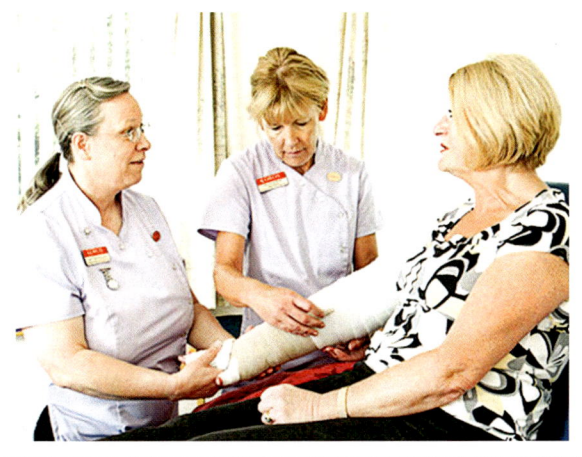

Lymphoedema Clinic

distress. It may affect the wearing of normal clothing and footwear, thus preventing the patient from going out, and depriving them of a normal social life. One patient found that, although suffering from Lymphoedema for thirty-eight years, after bandaging and massage treatment at the new LOROS Clinic, she lost two litres of liquid from her arm and was at last able to wear normal clothes again. In 2010 the Lymphoedema Clinic treated 254 new patients and gave 2,123 patients follow-up appointments.

In 2004, in response to the changing ethnic balance of Leicester's population, the first Cultural Support Worker was appointed. Anjana Vaja, a Hindhu, speaks Gujarati as well as fluent English and her role is to provide a link between the multi-disciplinary team and an Asian patient and their family. Although she can act as an interpreter if required, she prefers to talk direct to the patient. As there are now around one hundred languages spoken in Leicester, Anjana has compiled a Register of Interpreters, but this is costly to LOROS. For ward nurses she has designed small laminated language translation cards to fit in the pocket. On the ward she especially assists Asian families in three ways:– Firstly, with the dietary requirements of their faith (Muslims no pork, Sikhs and Hindhus no beef, Halal and Kosher) – a fear of breaking dietary rules may make a patient decline admission to the Hospice. Secondly, with facilitating their rituals for the dying, such as the administering of Holy Water from

Anjana Vaja, our first Cultural Support Worker, talks to a patient

the Wells of Mecca or the River Ganges, the chanting of prayers and the comfort of family shrines. And, thirdly, with strict religious post-death customs, particularly those governing the preparation of a body, and who is permitted to touch it. Anjana also accompanies the CNS Team into people's homes, and has devised and runs cultural awareness education programmes.

Of vital importance to a patient's sense of enjoyment of life is the quality, taste and variety of their food. Ever since 1985 the Hospice cook has been renowned for skill in creating high quality simple food, prepared and cooked on the premises, and served individually to patients by the catering staff. For David Forbes, Head Chef since 1991, nothing is too much trouble. A main meal with choices is served at midday, with an alcoholic drink or fruit juice offered beforehand. Special diets and cultural or religious dietary requirements are catered for, and vitamin-fortified drinks are turned into exciting cocktails, with such exotic names as 'Bubbly Booster', 'Desert Island Drifter' and 'Sunset Surprise'. A specially trained Ward Volunteer Team assists those patients who cannot feed themselves, helping them to maintain dignity at mealtimes. David also caters for those attending meetings and education courses at the Hospice, and puts on a sumptuous spread for the annual Hospice Volunteers Party. Birthday cakes are produced, and more poignant parties for Hospice weddings, blessings and christenings catered for.

David Forbes, Head Chef since 1991

One family held a splendid 18th birthday party just days before the young patient died. In fact, David will provide virtually anything that a dying patient requests – a favourite dish of tripe not tasted since childhood; a Chinese meal; ice cream for breakfast – and even champagne for a patient who had never tasted it before!

The hygiene and freshness of the ward and its surroundings also enhances the patient's Hospice experience. Manager Di Linley employs, supervises and trains her team of sixteen domestic staff, who rotate their work in every area of the Hospice. This enables them to get to know patients and families and they take great joy in making them comfortable. Di explains that now many patients are coming in to the ward in the later stages of illness, there is even more need for caring, kindness and consideration. In her words, "we must never lose 'care' – either for each other or for our patients."

To further this important aim of 'caring for each other', a Practice Development Team was set up in 2006, to nurture the physical and emotional care of the ward nursing staff. It works one-to-one with them in order to increase their confidence and help them to feel valued, and it acknowledges the emotional burden which working in hospice care can carry. The Team also assists nurses to develop effective coping skills, facilitating expression of feeling in a safe and supportive environment, and helps them devise their own professional development plans.

And on a more practical front, the Administration Team, headed by Manager Kim Fowler, has over the last ten years greatly improved patient documentation, making it considerably easier for medical staff to access vital information. The old hand-written paper records have been replaced by sophisticated IT systems that link up with the local hospitals, and will soon also connect with GP records. Kim encourages her staff to support each other, as well as showing consideration to patients and families – so all her Team attend in-house courses in communication skills.

So what are the principal changes in LOROS patient care and services over the years? When Matron Chris arrived in 2001 legislation and regulation were beginning to change. The Care

Quality Commission is now the legislative body that regulates LOROS, ensuring that the requirements of the Care Standards Act (2000) and the Health and Social Care Act (2008) are embraced and implemented. Additionally the Health and Safety regulations, particularly around the management of drugs and monitoring of infections, sees LOROS increasingly burdened with legislation and bureaucracy, and the demands of working with Primary Care Trusts. But LOROS can be immensely proud of the many positive developments in patient care during the last ten years; the more complex though still intensely loving care given to much sicker patients; the 18%-20% of seriously ill patients who now access the ward out-of-hours; the end-of-life care offered for other illnesses besides cancer; and the continual development of skills and knowledge of the committed nursing staff. To support all this work, there are now more staff on the ward than in the early years, but this larger team is as dedicated as ever.

Looking back over the quarter century, Senior Ward Sister, Wendy Taylor, a devoted LOROS nurse since its very first year, reflects, "twenty-five years ago we were a nurse led unit. We have seen an ever increasing number of medical interventions, such as blood transfusions and intravenous drips, and the challenge now is to retain a balance between embracing new sophisticated treatments and technical advances without diluting the founding principles of compassionate, holistic care." On reading a very early LOROS newsletter, it seems that, despite the organisation's quarter century of substantial development and expansion, its simple message remains the same. For in 1985 a LOROS observer wrote that – 'care is centred on the patient and aimed at enhancing the quality of life by relieving painful symptoms, by sharing difficulties with both patient and family, and by offering simple human friendship against a backdrop of professional skills.' All of these tenets remain today. As one LOROS patient recalled with some emotion, "I arrived a stranger and left as a friend."

CHAPTER FOUR
SPIRITUAL, EMOTIONAL AND THERAPEUTIC CARE

In 1985 Ward Sister Jean Riley, newly arrived at LOROS, yearned to provide 'a better way of dying'. She saw that the social, spiritual and emotional needs of both the patient and the family were equally as important as their physical needs. LOROS provided Spiritual Care and Counselling from the very start, and has added complementary therapies and other holistic treatments over the period of twenty-five years.

Spiritual Care and Chaplaincy

The original Hospice building included a Chapel, and at the outset various part-time Anglican Hospice chaplains were funded by the Diocese of Leicester. But in 1991 Reverend Kenneth Cook, was appointed the first full-time Co-ordinating Chaplain, assisted by two additional part-time clergy from other denominations, with input from religious leaders of other faiths, and some 'out-of-hours' cover from Glenfield Hospital Chaplaincy. Catholic priest, Father Joe Carty, brought support and humour to the Hospice Chaplaincy from 1985 to 2001 and Free Church Chaplain, Reverend Jean Wileman, also joined the team in 1985 and gave eleven years service.

From 1997-2003 Reverend Joy Chapman was Co-ordinating Chaplain, and during her time the Chaplaincy became really well established, with regular Sunday Services, bedside ministry for the very sick, and pastoral care given to everyone, whatever their beliefs. Joy aimed to assist patients in living life to its fullest and to help them to face their own dying. Sometimes a patient might wish to be baptized, confirmed or married and she would arrange and administer these, and was often involved in funeral planning. She once conducted a Pre-Wedding Service for a bride whose very ill mother would not live to attend the actual wedding. She liaised with both nursing and counselling teams, and would make herself available immediately a person had died, or would say prayers of commendation with the family at the time of passing. Joy visited Manor Croft once a week and whilst there included thoughts and prayers for recently deceased patients. She compiled a list of resources for the other principal faiths, whose Holy Books and artefacts can be borrowed from the Chapel and used on the ward. Perhaps her most creative task was a Service of Blessing for Smudge, the deceased but much-loved Hospice cat!

'Light up a Tree', the 'In Memory' Christmas Tree, was first introduced in 1995, but with Joy it became a much larger, more significant and moving outdoor event attended by several thousand people. It soon became known as 'Light up a Life'. During the Service, after a moment of silence, the lights suddenly blaze out – a magical and spiritual experience for everyone, and a source of strength to the bereaved. In 1999 Joy also set up twice-yearly Services of Thanksgiving and Remembrance, to which all recently bereaved families of those who have died at the Hospice are invited. They can light their own Chapel candle, look at the Book of Remembrance, and talk with staff, volunteers and other bereaved families.

Reverend Helen Newman, Co-ordinating Chaplain since 2009, works with a team of five chaplains from the Church of England, Catholic and Free Churches – both paid and volunteers. Together

First ever 'Light up a Tree' service 1995

the chaplains seek to provide continuous cover for the pastoral, spiritual and religious needs of Hospice and Manor Croft patients, their families and staff – those of all faiths and of none. Volunteer chaplains from the Muslim, Hindu, Jewish and Sikh communities are part of the wider team and will visit patients at an individual's request. Helen has introduced 'Soul Space', a calm and peaceful 15-minute Thursday lunchtime slot for staff, both Christian and non-Christian. Because many in-Hospice patients are now much sicker, there are no regular Sunday chapel services, and much of Helen's ministry is in the ward, at the bedside, and with families and staff. She is there for those who come in to the Chapel to light a candle or write in the Memorial Book, and attends daily to prayer requests placed in the Prayer Box.

Counselling Service

In the early 1980s the very concept of counselling was new. But LOROS straight away recognised its importance in caring for the terminally ill and their families, and appointed Mrs Derri Robson-Dixé, a Senior Psychiatric Social Worker, as the first Honorary Director of its new Counselling Service. This started in a small way and advice was obtained from other hospices. Volunteer counsellors were gradually trained and had to gain experience in counselling terminally ill patients and their relatives, and counselling the bereaved following a death. In June 1984 the first patient was referred, and the Service was run from the first floor at Manor Croft until transferring to the new Hospice in 1985. By the following year ninety clients had been seen.

In 1988 Lizette Pugh became the first paid Head of Counselling, with a team of around twenty carefully selected fully trained volunteers, working in the small Hospice counselling room, or at the patient's bedside, in the children's playroom, or at people's homes. Lizette ran all the LOROS training courses, and also became involved in many aspects of counselling outside, travelling, lecturing, and running courses for volunteers and professionals elsewhere. The Counselling Service paid particular attention to the emotional and practical needs of young parents and their families, and might assist in breaking sad news to children. To celebrate the 10th Anniversary of the Service a Birthday Party for LOROS bereaved children was given, complete with games, tea, birthday cake and a magic man. Afterwards, one mother wrote of her joy at seeing her children's sad eyes become sparkling with fun again just for a short while.

Simon Bellham took the helm in 1995, when he put a more formal structure in place. A significant change was for a much smaller team of counsellors, who were all paid and more or less full-time. In 2000 Rosemarie Freer, already an experienced counsellor and an early Voluntary Services Co-ordinator at Manor Croft, became Counselling Manager. In this role Rosemarie continues to carry out administration and counselling, organises external study days, and attends conferences at other hospices. She has developed ward counselling, working alongside nurses and doctors who are quick to identify a need; and also acts as a facilitator with couples and family relationships, assisting them to sort out, improve and open up their feelings, and tackle significant and meaningful issues during the last weeks of a loved one's life.

Complementary therapies

There are a number of other ways in which all-embracing care at LOROS has been realized over the last quarter century, helping patients to make the most of each and every day. Hairdressing, beauty and manicure care were given by volunteers from the very

Senior Sister/Manager of the Complementary Therapy Team talks to a patient

early days, and at Manor Croft the 1990 extension provided the extra space for a Hairdressing and Beauty Salon. At the Hospice a gentleman barber regularly gave up his Wednesday half-day closing afternoons to cut patients' hair. Complementary therapies, such as Reflexology and Hypnotherapy, were first offered by ward nurses who were keen to find additional ways of bringing comfort and well-being to their patients. Then in 1989 Nurse Alison Roe gained a Diploma in Aromatherapy and a Massage Clinic for both ward and home care patients was set up. Alison explained "Massage has many benefits. On a physical level it can relieve pain, ease tension and tight muscles and increase circulation; on an emotional level, it is soothing, warming, very relaxing and gives a sense of well-being." In 1991 the LOROS physiotherapist was able to use donations to purchase acupuncture needles and pain-relieving TENS machines to further assist patients' comfort.

But real strides forward were made in 2001 when the spacious new Hospice extension included a specifically dedicated Complementary Therapies Room. Imagery, Relaxation, Massage, Aromatherapy and Reflexology could now be given by specialist practitioners, with one-to-one attention giving patients a warm feeling of self-worth and well-being. In 2009/10 a total of 878 therapy sessions were carried out, and in 2011 any known LOROS patient can avail themselves free of charge of six 45-minute sessions of Aromatherapy, Reflexology, Indian Head Massage, Relaxation & Visualisation, or Hypnosis. The team of four part-time trained therapists, one volunteer and a co-ordinator, are able to enhance the quality of life by providing a safe environment in which to relax and chat. And ever-willing volunteers continue to give pleasure with their specialist skills in hairdressing, beautician and manicure services.

Nature, Animals, Reminiscences, Art
On entering the Hospice, the visitor is immediately assailed by an atmosphere of peacefulness; a sense of the natural world and calm. Simple but tasteful furnishings and fabrics, quiet rooms, gentle colours, restful and nostalgic pictures, all soothe the spirit. Luxuriant flower arrangements brighten the air with colour and sweet smells, and water pools and fountains surrounded by shady green plants induce a feeling of tranquillity. In the central quadrangle garden

are wooden seats, trees, shrubs, a pool with fish, and an aviary of budgerigars that fills the air with birdsong. The aviary, erected in 1989, originally stood alongside the social area, but was re-located when the children's play area was formed nearby. The connectedness of gardens and ward greatly enhances the well-being of patients and their families, and is a tribute to the LOROS landscape gardeners and their hard-working volunteers.

Dr Sam Ahmedzai, first LOROS Medical Director, was a great believer in the therapeutic value of animals. As a consequence, LOROS patients have always been allowed, and even encouraged, to have their pets visit them. And the ward itself has had several pets – Angel, the pure white Canary who sat at the nurses' station, arrived almost at the start, and Smudge came as a kitten in 1987. He soon became part of the ward, nestling down on the beds of extremely ill patients, seeming to instinctively know who needed that extra cuddle, comfort and reassurance. The Hospice was one

Early days: Wendy Taylor with a patient and Smudge, the cat

of the first palliative care units in the country to initiate a Pat Dog Scheme. Honey, a very friendly and docile golden Labrador, visited patients and staff twice a week with her owner. Honey was presented to the Prince and Princess of Wales at the Official Opening, and featured in the video, as well as in several others films made for the medical profession. Bonney, a black Flatcoat Retriever succeeded Honey, and Greyhound Max, who had formerly been ill-treated and starved, grew to be loving when stroked by patients. Tina, a mongrel Terrier whose owner had died at the Hospice, was adopted by a Ward Nurse Volunteer, and visited with her each week. And Pat Dog Gunner visited weekly for ten years and was eventually replaced by Robin.

The process of looking back can often bring comfort and peace of mind to those nearing the end of life. In 2005 a dedicated group of staff developed a 'Reminiscence Corner' in the social area of the in-patient unit, that has featured such topics as Autumn, The Seaside,

'Pat Dog' with volunteer at Christmas time

Winter, and Valentine's Day. Reminiscence can be described as the process of recalling and sharing one's memories, helping people to review their life in a positive way. It encourages communication and social interaction and enhances people's sense of identity and self worth.

Art and Creative Therapy is yet another way in which patients draw strength, and emotional and spiritual fulfillment, during the last period of their life. In 1988 Margaret Gold, a qualified art therapist and member of the LOROS Counselling Service, set up the LOROS Art Therapy Service. She said "Being involved in art enables the patient to focus on something other than their illness. The patients' emotions are given a natural release, and their work can express many intense feelings whether of shock, fear, anger, loss or sadness, and equally, of hope, gratitude, courage, faith, love and joy." Many patients derived enormous benefit and pleasure from this diversion, that included painting, drawing, making items out of wood, producing tapestry and embroidery. When after eighteen years Margaret retired from LOROS, a permanent Creative Therapist was appointed, who runs sessions every day. A smiling patient reflected that "creative therapy focuses the mind on what you can do, rather than what you can't."

With this comprehensive range of imaginative holistic activities, LOROS has certainly achieved its early dream of providing 'a better way of dying'.

Art Therapy at Manor Croft

Dreams come true

At LOROS fostering the hopes and goals of patients is also essential. And every so often the multi-disciplinary team works its magic and makes a special dream come true.

Ada, a 76-year old cancer sufferer, who had never flown in an aeroplane before, was escorted by a LOROS officer on a non-stop flight to Glasgow and back, in the best seats, and with all in-flight luxuries of food and drink free of charge.

Ada gives a happy wave

Matron secured tickets for Michael, a Hospice In-patient, to attend the 1991 Wembley Cup Final, to watch his favourite team Nottingham Forest. Michael, Nurse, medicine and wheelchair were all taken to Wembley in the Day Centre minibus, decorated in red and white streamers and balloons by family and Hospice staff.

Manor Croft patient, Jack, travelled to London to achieve a life long ambition – to watch a match at Lords cricket ground. Jack and a LOROS Nursing Officer travelled first class by train and had prime tickets in the ground.

Jane died just a week after sharing in the baptism of her eleven year old daughter, Nichola, in the LOROS chapel, and surrounded by family, godparents, patients, staff and visitors.

Nichola Jayne is baptised at LOROS

Martin, just twenty-one years old and suffering with a severe brain tumour, saw Leicester City win at Wembley and go into the Premier Division. All the effort was worthwhile just to see the joy and tears on his face as Steve Claridge scored the winning goal.

Martin looking forward to seeing Leicester City

Bharti brought forward her wedding, so that she could receive her bed-ridden Dad's blessing just before he passed away. LOROS staff pulled out all the stops and arranged for a priest and flowers at a few hours notice. Bharti's father gave his blessing and had kept his promise to his daughter to be present - but died later that same day.

The happy couple

Manor Croft patient, Janet, attended London's glittering Ritz Hotel in London when actress, Jane Asher, hosted a very special celebrity tea party. Janet recalled "Jennie Bond was the first celebrity guest to welcome me with a glass of champagne whilst a musician played the grand piano."

Janet enjoying tea at the Ritz with Jennie Bond

A young patient's favourite musical was 'Beauty and the Beast', so a travelling theatre company brought its performance to the Hospice seminar room, where audience members became puppeteers and actors – and much enjoyment was had by all.

LOROS's philosophy is to actively encourage living and celebration of life even through the hardest time of one's life.

CHAPTER FIVE
CARE IN THE COMMUNITY

There are three LOROS strands that operate beyond the Hospice – the Manor Croft Day Therapy Unit; the Community Nurse Specialist Team; and the Family Support Service. Hospice-at-Home started life at LOROS but is now independently run.

Manor Croft Day Therapy Unit

Everything done at Manor Croft is to re-affirm living, rather than dying, and every effort is made to enhance the quality of life. Manor Croft, a spacious family house in the leafy suburbs of Leicester, was purchased as a LOROS Day Centre in 1983, so that terminally ill patients could receive support even before the Hospice was built,

Anne Kind OBE and Phina Johnson cut Manor Croft 25th anniversary cake

and in order that the generous people of Leicestershire could see their donations being put to good use. The first Manor Croft patient was received on 18th April 1984 and in June the Lord Mayor, Councillor Michael Cufflin OBE, officially opened the Day Centre. Mr Alan Hopkinson became Chairman of the newly-formed Manor Croft Management Committee, succeeded by Dr Bill Kind, a prodigious 'handyman' and all-round helper. Mrs Phina Johnson, an SRN specially qualified in caring for the terminally ill, was the first Officer in Charge until 1999, and Mrs Dorothy Rice was the first Social Worker. The LOROS Counselling Service started life from here until it was transferred to the new Hospice. The Day Centre initially catered for fifteen patients, until the extension of 1990 increased the numbers to a maximum of twenty-five. By 1988 ninety-six volunteers were assisting, thirty-nine of whom were drivers ferrying patients to and from home, and clocking up 2,000 miles a month. And from the outset Women's Institute volunteers were filling the Manor Croft freezers with mouth-watering cakes and goodies.

The whole ethos of Manor Croft is that of a warm, friendly and welcoming 'home', rather than a hospital. Patients can socialise with

Staff and volunteers at Manor Croft

others with similar problems, or unburden their feelings to the open ears of staff or volunteers. They can enjoy a glass of sherry and a tasty home-cooked lunch, sit in the tranquil gardens, play games, engage in art or creative therapy, listen to music, and benefit from hairdressing, manicures, beauty care – and a walk-in bath! Day trips out might include visits to gardens, a pub lunch, a concert, the seaside, or a pleasant canal trip organised by the Peter Le Marchant Trust. Many birthday parties are celebrated at the Therapy Unit, and highlights of the year are the Summer Garden Fete, the Annual Grand Raffle, and the special Manor Croft Christmas. Tinsel is hung, the Christmas tree decorated, cards exchanged and carols sung; and a lavish Christmas luncheon is followed by crackers and a special gift from Santa.

But in addition to all this fun, on each visit qualified nursing staff monitor a Manor Croft patient's well-being, attending to symptom control, medication, or the renewal of dressings. It also offers a patient's carer a much-needed 'day off'. Manor Croft also welcomes those suffering from the devastating effects of Motor Neurone Disease (MND) and in 2006 LOROS secured a grant to fund a MND Project Worker. The widow of an MND patient observed "through MND we both made many wonderful friends and were given every possible help." In 1995 a Younger Person's Day', for those under the age of fifty, was set up at Manor Croft, where alternative and art therapies are available, social activities, relaxation classes, games and music enjoyed – or it is just a special day to rest and chat with like-minded friends. A bereaved daughter confided to the Therapy Unit staff that, "despite her illness, there was much happiness in the last few months of Mum's life, and this was due mainly to the time she spent at Manor Croft."

Community Nurse Specialist Team
(formerly Home Care Service)

Home Care was introduced in the very early LOROS years by Matron Bronwen, and the initial group was known as 'Home Care Sisters'. In 1990 a Home Care Team was established on a more formal basis and consisted of a Senior Sister, Home Care Sister, Dr Ian Johnson, and input from the Chaplain, Social Worker and Physiotherapist. Its tasks were two-fold – to provide a link for patients alternating between Hospice and home, and to visit those referred to LOROS for symptom control whilst remaining at home. The Team worked in conjunction with Macmillan nurses, who were usually the first to visit patients in their home, with the LOROS Team following on.

In 1999 the Home Care Service consisted of five Sisters who between them carried out over 2,500 visits a year. Housed in a Portakabin outside the Hospice building, they were looking forward to moving to their much-needed Home Care Suite in the proposed major Hospice extension. Following NHS changes the same year, the Nursing Development Unit (NDU) was developed that saw LOROS and Macmillan Teams working together. And in 2002 this joint NDU was the first Community Team in the whole UK to be awarded a formal accreditation. Then known as the LOROS Clinical Nurse Specialist Team (CNS), the nurses developed a trusting relationship with patients and carers throughout the illness. They were skilled at pre-empting a medical crisis before it occurred, and would liaise with a patient's GP on the most suitable and effective medication.

The CNS team in 2006

An exciting new initiative was 'nurse prescribing' and in 2002 three of the CNS Team became qualified to prescribe drugs for patients without having to refer to GPs, saving much time and patient anxiety. In 2007 there were eight nurses in what had now received the name of Community Nurse Specialist Team (CNS) (its fourth change of title!). The Team continued to work in conjunction with Macmillan Nurses (funded by NHS) and the highly supportive District Nurses. The CNS Team had the input, if needed, of the LOROS Cultural Support Worker, and was ably supported by an Adminstrator, Secretary, and an excellent group of volunteers. By 2009 the CNSs were visiting the homes of around 700 patients each year, that included some with other life-limiting conditions; they were giving thoughtful support if a patient's family included young children; could provide advice on the benefits system, and on LOROS and other services; and gave help after a bereavement. In 2011 all the CNS Team are Prescribers, and with the introduction of Gold Standards Meetings, they once a month attend multi-disciplinary meetings at GP surgeries, and work with patients and doctors towards planning End-of-Life Strategies. But perhaps the Team's greatest gift is to make the patient and family feel that they are no longer alone.

Family Support Service
(formerly Volunteer Sitting Service)

Until the LOROS Sitting Service started in 1992, many carers who looked after their terminally ill relatives 24 hours a day experienced profound feelings of isolation, anxiety and loss of freedom. By 1998 a group of forty trained Volunteer Sitters, co-ordinated by Margaret Geary, were minding patients whilst their hard-working carers took a much-needed break; or were giving sociable company to patients who lived alone. In addition a LOROS Befriending Service gave short-term companionship to members of the family. Then weekly Carers' Group Meetings were started up at the Hospice, where carers could draw comfort from exchanging viewpoints with each other, and also receive practical advice and information.

In due course some paid ex-nurses and mental health care professionals joined the team, and the volunteer sitters were given a higher level of support and training, because it was realized that many family relationships are complex and sometimes hard to deal with. In addition Befriending Service volunteers might accompany patients and carers on home visits or to hospital appointments, or just sit comfortingly at the bedside of a very poorly Hospice patient. By 2003 another strand of support was initiated, when it was realized that a bereaved carer had suffered not only the loss of their loved one, but also the ongoing company and support of the Sitting and Befriending Services. So a Bereavement Visiting Service was set up, to give friendship to bereaved carers for up to four hours a week for a maximum of twelve weeks, to tide them over that very difficult time. At this point, the three groups were amalgamated to form the Family Support Service (FSS). In 2011 a management of four healthcare professionals runs the FSS visiting team of thirty, that includes six volunteers. Their training includes communication skills, food hygiene, back awareness, and vulnerable adults directives, and they have all developed a high level of expertise to meet the needs of patients in the community.

Hospice-at-Home and Motor Neurone Disease Support

The Hospice-at-Home (HatH) Project was developed jointly between LOROS and the NHS Healthcare Trust in 2001. Mirroring similar schemes in other parts of the country, it provided hospice care to patients in their own homes. It started in a small way with just a project manager and three nurses, covering only the city of Leicester, but linking closely with existing services such as the LOROS Sitting Service and the Marie Curie Service. HatH was initially based at the Hospice, but has since moved to Barrow-on-Soar, though it still maintains close links with LOROS. A Motor Neurone Disease (MND) Team with two CNSs has an office and a Clinic at the Hospice, but is not funded by LOROS.

CHAPTER SIX
EDUCATION AND RESEARCH

Education and training has been at the heart of the LOROS endeavour from the very start, and has taken two forms – firstly, the education of its own staff, professionals and volunteers; and, secondly, the dissemination of knowledge and expertise to health and social care workers of all levels amongst the wider community.

Even in the early days all staff were given tuition in communication skills; volunteers were trained in the various aspects of their work; volunteer counsellors were taught their skills at LOROS; Sitting Service volunteers received very comprehensive instruction; and (from 1989) all LOROS shop volunteers were given training. Soon after opening, the Hospice set up educational programmes for district nurses and GPs in the administration of pain-killing drugs, with a six-weeks course in palliative care for nurses. LOROS was acquiring its expertise from other hospices and, through education courses, was effectively handing it on to healthcare professionals within the wider community. Student nurses and medical students gained valuable experience from placements on the ward. Dr Ahmedzai travelled a great deal to speak at conferences and doctors came to LOROS from abroad to learn the new palliative care skills. By 1996 LOROS was training Senior Registrar doctors in Palliative Medicine, and students of radiotherapy, pharmacy and nursing home staff were also attending courses at the Hospice.

However in 2002 LOROS set up a more formal education programme. It was run initially by Head of Education, Sharon de Caestecker, but within a short period of time was supported by a social worker and an occupational therapist. Since then this department has grown and expanded considerably, and its aim is to develop competence and confidence in all students. It now has sixteen paid staff, and runs almost daily educational courses at the Hospice and at various Healthcare Centres throughout the county. In addition four Practice Development Team members go out into practical situations and work alongside staff in hospitals and care homes. The CNS Team offers training to patients and families, and to health and social care professionals. The LOROS Chaplain gives guidance on spiritual care to staff, student nurses and at De Montfort University School of Nursing (DMUSN). The Cultural Awareness Officer educates LOROS staff and volunteers and District Nurses within the community, runs a twice-a-year language workshop at the Hospice, an annual course at DMUSN, and responds to requests for cultural awareness training from other agencies. In 2007 the LOROS Education Department invited patients and carers to share their own first-hand experiences with healthcare professionals, as a further valuable means of extending training.

At the present time doctors at many levels benefit greatly from various LOROS Palliative Medicine training programmes. All University of Leicester medical students spend two days at the Hospice; all newly qualified doctors are taught in their own hospital by a LOROS Consultant; there are usually three junior doctors on the LOROS ward, working in four-month blocks, as well as four or five full-time Registrar doctors wishing to make their career in Palliative Medicine. Two LOROS Consultants visit the 150 GP practices in Leicestershire and Rutland, to engage in discussions and exchange knowledge and expertise.

In 2007 a Foundation Degree in Palliative and Supportive Care developed by LOROS was the first of its kind in the whole world. A mix of academic and vocational learning, it is aimed at health and social care support staff wishing to further develop their skills, and positively recognises their key role across all settings. Attracting a good deal of interest both regionally and nationally, the first students of this innovative course graduated in July 2009. The Education Department also runs a twelve-module Post Graduate Masters course, and has recently embarked on an education initiative with the Decisions at End-of-Life project to improve communication skills, involving role play, video feedback and professional actors. At the present time LOROS education is bringing skills and a greater understanding of palliative care to around 1,500 healthcare professional delegates a year, thus enriching the end-of-life experience for many local people.

Research was embedded from the start in the founding mission of LOROS. In 1990 Dr Ahmedzai published one of the first studies looking at the work of hospices, and went on to develop a holistic research programme, ranging from the effects of companion animals on quality of life to comparison of drug treatments for pain and other symptom management. LOROS has also been involved with many local academics and has participated in studies such as looking at the experience of living with, and the psychological effect of, advanced cancer. Decision making in advanced illness is a complex business, and LOROS is currently engaged in research projects regarding matters such as resuscitation, organ and tissue donation, and responding to a patient's request to withdraw supportive ventilation.

LOROS education and research programmes are enabling the Organisation to achieve even greater support and comfort for its patients – those people who are undergoing an experience common to all human beings, the end-of-life experience; and with LOROS's help it is constantly becoming a better experience.

Students taking the Foundation degree in Palliative and Supportive Care

CHAPTER SEVEN
VOLUNTEERS

Volunteers have been at the very heart of the LOROS endeavour ever since the first suggestions for a Leicestershire Hospice were voiced. Without volunteers the LOROS concept could never have been developed and brought to fruition. A great debt of gratitude is owed to these people, men and women, young and old, rich and poor, from city and county, and from all walks of life, who twenty-five years ago had the vision, perseverance and courage to create what is today the astonishing LOROS achievement.

The very first LOROS newsletter circulated to the community in 1978 carried an appeal for potential volunteers, and soon a register was compiled. When in 1981 Anne Kind began work as Administrator, she immediately set about inaugurating a scheme for volunteers, whose service was essential if the LOROS dream were to become a reality. The news spread like wildfire, and people began flocking to Anne's tiny office to offer voluntary help of many different kinds. Initially there were four principal tasks:- to raise funds, to form local Support Groups, to give county-wide talks on LOROS, and to assist Anne with clerical work.

Queniborough Support Group with Lady Gretton

The first fundraising efforts put on by volunteers included a Flag Day, Magic Evening, Cookery Demonstration, Sponsored Fishing Marathon, Fashion Show, Barn Dance, Football Match, Craft Market and Flower Arranging Demonstration. But perhaps the most daring event was the sponsoring of drinkers to 'Down a Pint of Beer in 30 Seconds'! The first promotional goods sold by volunteers were pens, keyrings and bookmarks, but within two years a range of twenty such items had been developed to proclaim the LOROS message. Dedicated helpers re-vamped old Christmas cards to sell the following year. Ardent volunteers delivered collecting boxes to shops, or undertook house-to-house collections. And a spirited team of volunteer fundraisers drove around in a rickety old bus attending local events, where they sold goods to raise funds, told people about the new LOROS project, and recruited more volunteers. For the 1984 Phase II LOROS Appeal, it was decided that local businesses should be approached, and volunteers known as 'Cash Commandos' were recruited who each tackled five or six businesses. Several major fundraising events, inaugurated very early on by volunteers, are still key fundraisers today, such as the Houghton-Keyham Christmas Walk (1982), the Tennis Tournaments (1984) and Ladies Luncheon (1984). The Summer Fair (1987), that was planned, set up and run entirely by volunteers, became increasingly more elaborate and successful, and the last one staged in 2001 raised £92,000.

In 1981 the notion of volunteer Support Groups was quick to catch on, and within the first fifteen months forty-one such groups were set up throughout the locality. By September 1982 £210,000 had been raised entirely through the efforts of volunteer workers, and in Spring 1983 £330,000 towards the £1½ million target had been realised. From the outset volunteers had given talks on LOROS, but in 1984 a more formal LOROS Panel of Speakers was set up, co-ordinated by Dr Edna Clitheroe. These fifteen feisty volunteers were given training to develop professional public speaking skills, and they went out and addressed medical groups, industry, W.I.s, church groups, Rotary Clubs, schools and other interested parties. Pressure of work was mounting for the volunteer administration staff, and when in 1983 the Appeals Office moved to its more spacious premises in Welford Road, additional voluntary clerical staff were recruited.

With the opening in 1984 of the Manor Croft Day Centre, the first opportunities arose for voluntary work with patient contact. Now as then, volunteers look after patients' needs, making teas, coffees, serving lunch and clearing away. Others help in the kitchen, do some ironing, attend to the flowers, and during the afternoon play cards, Scrabble or dominoes with their guests. Volunteers act as drivers, collecting and returning day patients, and also accompany them on a variety of pleasant outings. Two people who have given their services voluntarily at Manor Croft over the years are the pianist who entertains delighted audiences with light music and carols at Christmastime; and the art therapist who brought joy and fulfillment to day patients for eighteen years. And of course the LOROS counsellors, originally based at Manor Croft, worked as volunteers for the first decade of the Service.

When the main Hospice opened in 1985, Margaret Kirby, the newly-appointed and inspirational Volunteer Co-ordinator, worked prodigiously to recruit voluntary helpers for Hospice work as well. Amongst those who offered were the wives of men in Rotary Clubs,

Manor Croft volunteer Evelyn Hawkes receiving her 25 year service badge from Stephen Thomas, Chairman of Trustees in 2009

Masons, and other such male groups involved in the Building Appeal fundraising, who had heard of the need for volunteers from their husbands. Within a few weeks 150 applicants had been accepted, were given an Induction Course, and had set to work, talking and reading with patients, doing their personal laundry, ironing and sewing, and arranging Hospice flowers. Soon bi-monthly Volunteer Meetings brought both social and practical benefits, and enthusiastic volunteers set about running the new Hospice snack bar, serving refreshments and making sandwiches and bringing in homemade cakes, manning Reception and acting as drivers. Volunteers had by now become indispensible and permeated every LOROS happening. They did clerical work, brought in pets for patients to 'pat', dug the new Hospice garden and raised money for the garden tools, attended to the aviary and fish ponds, recycled thousands of Christmas cards, and trailed the Manor Croft mobile shop around fetes and coffee mornings. And some retired trained nurses, and others with nursing-related experience, offered valuable hours on the ward as Nurse Volunteers. Perhaps one of the most unusual but commendable volunteer tasks was that of a calligraphist and a book binder, who for seventeen years between them diligently produced the Hospice Books of Remembrance. One of the most touching tasks was when a volunteer driver was asked to take an in-patient back to see his home for the very last time.

"Manning" the hospice snack bar

The volunteers' energy was indefatigable; their skills, confidence and competence ever burgeoning. Many of them were discovering latent talents that had lain dormant but were now bursting forth to serve the LOROS cause. For them it became a time of joy, self-discovery and personal development. These happy people were thrice rewarded; once in serving LOROS, secondly in the making of new meaningful friendships, and yet again through their own sense of fulfillment and achievement. And all around the county the active Support Groups bound communities together in enterprise, comradeship, fun – and fatigue! – through mad, daring, or just sensibly profit-making fundraising events. The inmates at Gartree Prison gave their best by making teddy bears for LOROS to sell; a reminder that volunteering can be for absolutely anybody.

In the decade 1987–1997 two major changes re-focussed the efforts of volunteer fundraising. Firstly, in 1987 Carole Wood was appointed full-time Liaison and Appeals Organiser, which meant that a professional team would now lead much of the fundraising effort, though ably supported by the volunteers of LOROS President Lady Palmer's Fundraising Committee. Secondly, in 1989 LOROS

LOROS shop volunteers at Birstall in 1995

opened the first of its twenty-one charity shops and in 1996 its LOROS Lottery scheme. The number of local Support Groups started to decline, but many new volunteers now joined to work in the shops and Lottery. In 1989 Co-ordinator Margaret Kirby retired, after a most successful career during which she had seen the number of volunteers grow to over 300. Beryl Chapman, with fifteen years experience co-ordinating staff at Marks and Spencer, then took over the Co-ordinator role, and after just a year in post she wrote that she was "overwhelmed by the support and unstinting dedication of all LOROS volunteers." Beryl continues to be the backbone of Hospice volunteering today.

A new challenge for volunteers arose in 1992 with the founding of the LOROS Volunteer Sitting Service. This scheme, co-ordinated by Margaret Geary, saw trained volunteers going into the home with the twofold objective of giving company and care to a patient, and giving their carer some much needed time out. As Margaret said "Volunteer Sitters not only give a lot to the patients they sit with, but get a lot in return, especially the satisfaction of knowing they are doing something worthwhile." By 1998 there were forty volunteer sitters but in recent years the issues have become more complex and now the team is made up of both professionals and volunteers (see page 46). 2005 was designated the 'Year of the Volunteer', and to mark this occasion LOROS Hospice volunteers compiled a stirring commemorative book of their memories over the previous twenty years.

Many people volunteer for LOROS because of a personal bereavement and, in recognition of what LOROS did for their loved-one, have a strong desire to give something back. This in turn can act as a balm to their grief and pain, and helps them to see some purpose in life again. Ann, a trained Lancôme beautician who had just lost her mother, gave up her Sunday mornings to open her 'Magic Box' of colours to beautify patients and uplift their spirits. Hairdresser Lesley, whose best friend had just died at LOROS, was at first apprehensive about styling patients' hair; but she soon discovered that she was gaining far more than she was giving. And recently-widowed Valerie found that working in a bright and sunny LOROS shop gave her the opportunity to meet and work with different people who took such pride in their store. And she came to see that both the Hospice and she had benefited from the experience. Julie volunteered as a Hospice receptionist following the funeral of a work colleague who had been a LOROS volunteer and then a Hospice patient. Julie joined the cheerful team who man the Reception desk every day from 8.30am-9.00pm. and welcome visitors with a friendly smile. They might direct visitors to a loved-one's bedside, make a cup of tea for an out-patient if they are early for an appointment, take business visitors to the offices, direct people to educational sessions, or take a newspaper to a patient's bedside. Sometimes bereaved children wish to repay LOROS for its loving care. When ten-year old Sandy's Mum, a long-term Hospice patient, died of cancer, he joined forces with another ten-year old who had lost an aunt to the disease. Together they sold LOROS cuddly toy seals at their primary school, organising it all themselves. They raised an impressive sum and proudly received a LOROS Certificate in School Assembly.

Hospice Reception Desk

In 2011 volunteers continue to act as drivers, flower arrangers, receptionists, snack bar servers and hairdressers. But they now also run the Hospice shop, do some light gardening and drive all around the county delivering thousands of cute LOROS cuddly toys. At Christmas time they hang the Hospice Christmas decorations and fill patients' Christmas stockings. And on Christmas Day volunteer helpers forego their own turkey lunches to ensure that the Hospice Reception is manned, and the patients get their mid-morning cup of tea. Volunteers support the medical team 365 day a year, and also help with the Lymphoedema Clinic and Complementary Therapy Services. Professional people volunteer their accounting and IT skills for the Finance and Administration Teams, the Education Department, or Community Nurse Specialist Team, while others assist with the filing of medical records. There are volunteer chaplains who move around the ward, offering support and following up with bereavement care when requested. Although there are now no Nurse Volunteers on the ward, a new Ward Volunteer Team was launched in 2010 to assist in ensuring that the nutritional needs of patients are met. One patient expressed to a Ward Volunteer that he would dearly love to eat a fish and chip meal just as he used to do, straight from the newspaper. The volunteer arranged this herself and the pair shared a fish and chip supper together, sitting by a seaside reminiscence display in the social area, with the music from 'Seaside Special' playing in the background.

Volunteers can claim expenses if they wish, in particular drivers who may obtain fuel money. Hospice and Manor Croft voluntary helpers are subject to the same strict interview process as paid employees; references and CRB checks are required and a check-up with Occupational Health for all drivers. They receive training in health and safety procedures, communication skills and cultural awareness, as well as for their own specialist tasks. Manor Croft volunteers come through the same central system run by the Volunteer Co-ordinator at the Hospice. There is no culture of 'us and them'; paid staff treat volunteers as equals, and greatly appreciate their considerable input. In 2011 twenty-eight volunteers work daily in the Hospice, and the service they give saves LOROS many thousands of pounds a year.

Personal fulfillment apart, there are a number of thoughtful ways that LOROS thanks and rewards its outstanding and committed team of volunteers. Service badges are given for five, ten, twenty and twenty-five years of all branches of LOROS volunteering. And great accent is put upon verbal thank-yous at all times. There is a Christmas Party every year to thank Hospice volunteers and acknowledge the value of their work, and this happy occasion provides an opportunity for the party-goers to share news and experiences. There is also 'royal' approval of LOROS voluntary work. Of the five volunteers who in 2011 had given twenty-five years service, two went to a Buckingham Palace Garden Party for the LOROS 20th Anniversary, and another two attended a Royal Garden Party for the 25th Anniversary. At the 2010 Opening of the new extension, several volunteers were presented to the Duchess of Gloucester, and the fifth volunteer with twenty-five years service was chosen to present the Duchess with a bouquet. In the same year, at a 'Help the Hospices' Silver Jubilee Reception at St James's Palace in London, Evelyn Hawkes, the longest serving LOROS volunteer, was presented to the Queen. Evelyn recounted that Her Majesty greeted her by name, chatted to her about her work at Manor Croft, and congratulated her on her 'long haul'.

Hospice 20th anniversary - two 20 year service lady volunteers are escorted to Buckingham Palace by two long serving Manor Croft gentlemen volunteers

CHAPTER EIGHT
FUNDRAISING

LOROS fundraising has during the past twenty-five years become a widespread and contagious local pastime. Why? – because anyone can do it! So how might one recognize these LOROS supporters? They are wise, focussed and generous hearted – and frequently innovative and fun-loving. The LOROS supporter could perhaps be divided into four archetypes: the individual; the family or friend-group; the formal LOROS Support Groups, local organisations and companies; and staff of the LOROS Fundraising Team and Shops and Lottery businesses.

The individual LOROS fundraiser might be someone who leaves the Hospice a legacy in their Will, buys a LOROS Lottery ticket or Christmas card, donates unwanted items for the shops, or undertakes a sponsored 'anything', from shaving their head to climbing the Great Wall of China. Some of the more unusual ways of raising much-needed LOROS funds have included a lady who knitted £650 worth of toys to sell for the cause; a gentleman who noted the mileage of his car and one year later later donated 1p for every mile driven; the pianist who raised over £1,000 to purchase a piano in order to entertain Hospice patients; and the florist who donates a bouquet each week to the top LOROS Lottery winner. In 2007 a local songwriter's composition 'Final Hope', written in memory of her father, a Hospice patient, was recorded by a Leicester Young Entertainer of the Year winner, and copies were sold for LOROS. And a Leicestershire man was so greatly moved by the story of a young and courageous dying LOROS patient that he started a Bird Box Campaign, selling personalised bird boxes and feeders for local nature sites, and raising around £10,000. Celebrity contributions have come from Leicester's Bishop Rutt, whose famous knitting patterns cost £1 per copy; and from Rosemary Conley who gave a percentage of the royalties from her 'Hip and Thigh Diet' book to Hospice funds.

Couples, families and friendship-groups are often motivated by the memory of a loved one when raising money for LOROS.

They frequently request donations to LOROS in lieu of funeral flowers, and even as early as 1986 £75,000 was raised by this means. Donations from couples have included a second marriage celebration, when LOROS donations were requested instead of wedding presents; a Golden Wedding couple who purchased one hundred gold LOROS pens to give to their guests; and a retired couple who gave LOROS part of their pension every six months for five years. Hundreds of coffee mornings, bazaars, concerts, craft or jumble sales, and sponsored activities have been undertaken by families and friendship-groups who feel deep personal gratitude to LOROS, including many young people and children. In 1982 a Market Harborough lady cajoled her friends into joining a LOROS Tennis Tournament, and soon more tennis groups were formed, so that fourteen years later a total of £43,000 had been raised. In more recent years two friends in Newbold Verdon have run a four-times-a year Stamp Collectors Fair, raising huge sums for LOROS. One of the most original fundraising schemes has to be the chums who gained sponsorship to drag a 12-ton longboat along a canal. But perhaps the quirkiest – and indeed the 'quackiest' – idea of all was the Birstall Duck Race. Visitors were enticed to spend £1 to enter one of the 3,000 plastic ducks in a neck-and-neck race on the River Soar at Birstall, and over a period of ten years the organising family handed over cheques to LOROS totalling £55,000.

The third category of LOROS fundraiser consists of LOROS Support Groups, charities, Rotary Clubs and Masons, sports, music and social clubs, schools, churches, and any kind of business. Even before the Hospice opened, LOROS encouraged and facilitated the setting up of county-wide Support Groups, that were created when a few enthusiastic friends formed a committee and organised events in their own village or area. By 1982 there were thirty-five such groups, and a year later their number had increased to sixty-four. Ten years on and the Support Groups were between them raising an annual sum of £70,000, through an endless round of coffee mornings, Bridge drives, cream teas, sponsored slims, swims, walks, runs, dances, jumble and car boot sales, garden parties and even a "Mr Blobby" knit-in! But in that same year it was costing £4 a minute to run LOROS services.

Local charities have made LOROS their Charity of the Year and several wealthy charitable trusts have donated a Manor Croft minibus. Golf, cricket, riding and football clubs have organised their own LOROS fundraising events, and local orchestras, choirs, bands, ensembles, jazz and opera groups have put on musical performances in aid of LOROS. Many dozens of social, cultural, and faith groups, functioning throughout Leicestershire and Rutland, have dreamed up imaginative or ingenious ways of acquiring a cheque for LOROS. And there is a special scheme for supplying bright ideas and publicity material to schools, colleges and universities who are keen to catch the LOROS bug. Businesses have given generous outright donations, or undertaken payroll giving or workplace group Christmas cards. Restaurants and theatres have run schemes to give LOROS a percentage of their takings, and a large Shopping Centre handed over £23,000-worth of coins that over three years had been thrown into its fountain. Friendship and work groups from all walks of life have participated in a huge variety of sponsored sporting challenges, from parachute and bunjee jumping, sky diving and abseiling to aerobics, swimming, cycling, bowling, dancing, marathon-running, dominoes and snooker. Enthusiastic clubs and societies have run

Margaret Kirby with BBC Radio Leicester presenter, Carolyn Oldershaw

bingo, quiz, disco or magic evenings; but the most fun and 'silly' events were perhaps the Wrinkly Ramblers Derbyshire Hike, the Midsummer Madness Knobbly Knees Competition, or the Fancy Dress Bike Ride around Rutland Water!

And finally the LOROS fundraising staff. Following the official Appeal Launch of March 1981, the earliest working party immediately swung vigorously into action. It was led by the recently-recruited paid Administrator, Anne Kind, who had just an Adler typewriter, a telephone, a small band of volunteers, and the guidance of a Fundraising Committee. Anne was dynamic in her leadership, energy and determination, and she worked ardently to inspire the people of Leicestershire to raise £1.5 million for their own Hospice. Her motto was 'Fundraising should be Fun'. By December 1983 £500,000 had been raised; Phase II, an Appeal to Industry, was launched in May 1984 and in March 1986 the full £1.5 million had been achieved. But the £330,00 sum for annual running costs also had to be met

Under Anne Kind's management, the next few years saw substantial income from 'In Memory' gifts, county-wide house-to-house collections, collecting boxes in shops, and donations in lieu of funeral flowers, whose 'thank you' scheme was ably administered by Mrs Dorothy Holmes. Big-money events put on by volunteers included an annual gymkhana, the Hinckley Metal Detectors competition, Mr and Mrs Paul Goodacres' yearly garden party, the Winter Sponsored Walk, and the 'Women of Achievement' Luncheon, soon re-named the LOROS Annual Ladies Luncheon. These last two are still big money-makers today. The former is a post-Christmas five-mile trek across the winter landscape from Houghton to Keyham and back, with hot soup and refreshments along the way; and the latter is the highly popular luncheon at which several hundred smartly-dressed ladies have over the years been entertained by such well-known celebrities as Lynda Lee-Potter, Roy Castle, Claire Rayner, Martin Bell, Earl Spencer, Peter Purves of 'Blue Peter' fame, and politician and 'dancer', Ann Widdecombe.

On Anne Kind's retirement in 1987, Carole Wood, a paid Liaison & Appeals Organiser, was appointed, and as Director of Appeals gave untiring and committed leadership to the Fundraising Team for thirteen years. 1987 also saw the first LOROS Summer Fair, held in the Hospice grounds. With its many colourful stalls and crafts, Grand Raffle, home-made jams, cakes and refreshments, brass bands and dance groups, clowns and stilt-walkers, barrel organ and Morris Men, pony rides and bouncy castle, it grew larger and more exciting every year for the next fifteen years. It was run mainly by LOROS volunteers, relatives, friends, staff, trustees and President, and many local businesses contributed. At this time LOROS President Lady Palmer also led her own committee of volunteer ladies who organised a number of prestigious and highly successful fundraising affairs, that included glamorous balls at Uppingham School, Belvoir Castle and Noseley Hall.

By 1990 the running costs of the growing LOROS enterprise had soared to £1.2 million. During the 1990s the professional Fundraising Team promoted the tax benefits of legacies, urged

Carole Wood organises a stall at Birstall

people to collect and send in their old or foreign coins, started the production of LOROS Christmas cards, and organised the popular Cathedral Christmas Concert. They enthusiastically engaged with the nation-wide Hospice Sunflower Appeal, when 50,000 Sunflower buttonholes were distributed, and they organised a number of enterprising 'Sunflower' events. The Millennium £1 million Hospice Building Project Appeal saw great generosity from local businesses, major charitable trusts and individual benefactors, but by now the annual running costs of the ever-expanding LOROS operation were £3 million.

During the decade of the 1990s two exciting new commercial enterprises were set up to boost much needed funds – the LOROS Shops and the LOROS Lottery. The first LOROS charity shop was opened in Loughborough in 1989, and since then one or two more shops have opened almost every year, so that in 2011 they number twenty-one (for a full list see page 20). Michael Archer, who came to LOROS in 1989 as General Manager, already had senior-level experience of running Oxfam charity shops. So he pioneered the LOROS Shops project, and Trading Manager, Jonathan Capewell, has run the operation with expertise and flair ever since. The first

Nigel Pearson, Leicester City Football Club's Manager, preparing for his Newcastle to Carlisle bike ride in 2010

shops sold only clothes and cards and there was an appeal to the general public to donate their used clothing. But over time some stores have become specialised – Oakham, in a town reputed for its antique and antiquarian book shops, sells collectables, bric-a-brac and books; Queen's Road, Leicester, situated near the University, has a highly popular second-hand book store; Uppingham Road, Leicester, has both a furniture shop and a media store, and at the latter customers often donate back used DVDs or books for further sale. Each shop has individuality in goods and style, as LOROS listens to what its customers want – an ethos that permeates the whole LOROS experience.

In the beginning Jonathan was the only salaried shops staff; he trained volunteers both in retailing, and for the office work that was carried out in a mobile classroom in the Hospice car park, with a garage at the Hospice acting as a warehouse for donated goods. In 1992 the shops acquired their own van, and then a second larger one for the collection of bulky furniture items. By the late 1990s the number of shops had increased again and there was now at least one paid staff in each shop. Since 2006 all shop tills have become computerised and Gift Aid on donated goods generates further income. In 2011 the shops employ fifty staff and have 550 volunteers. Annual sales are £2 million with a £0.6 million profit and around 300 bags of donated goods are received a day. Currently, extra revenue comes from the re-cycling of clothes, books and shoes. And volunteers sell specialist books on websites such as Amazon, and some exceptional donated items on E-Bay – including three cars! The highest priced item ever sold in a LOROS shop was a grandfather clock at the Oakham store, that fetched £1,500.

The idea of running a LOROS Lottery came from a Hospice in Preston, that LOROS had joined as a franchise, and then took up itself. The LOROS Lottery went public in July 1996. The first draw was launched at Manor Croft, assisted by the *Leicester Mercury*, and had about 2,000 members. Liz Singleton, Lottery Manager, felt drawn to this work because she had recently lost her mother to cancer, and has since then developed the project into a flourishing business. In 2011 the Lottery has 22,000 entries in its weekly draw and generates £0.7 million profit a year – the equivalent of the annual cost of twenty full-time LOROS nurses. There are around one hundred Lottery collectors, some paid, and others who wish to do the work voluntarily. There are three collection supervisors and in the Lottery office eleven paid staff and six volunteers. New ventures include a Telesales Lady inviting clients to take out a further card; Lottery scratch cards on sale at any LOROS shop, that are ideal as wedding favours or table gifts at parties and celebrations; and gift subscriptions to give as presents to family or friends. Amazingly, it still today only costs £1 for a Lottery ticket – the same price as when it started fifteen years ago. But the cost of running the Hospice continues to rise, so the Lottery must continually seek to increase its membership and the goodwill and assistance of its many customers and dedicated volunteer helpers.

During the 2000s LOROS Fundraising appointed a specialist to run its Making a Will Campaign; and a Corporate Fundraiser to engage with commerce and industry. Sponsorship for marathons became a popular money-raiser with LOROS supporters, who breathlessly tackled the Robin Hood Half Marathon, the Great North Run or the New York, London and Leicester Marathons.

Mrs Sue Murtha receiving a prize from Liz Singleton, Lottery Manager

Grand Raffle customers have been tempted with the top prize of a Nissan, Jaguar or Rover car, thanks to a generous local motor dealer; and November Fireworks Spectaculars at Stanford Hall, Mallory Park and Belvoir Castle have provided sparkling fun and funding. Other stirring events have been The Glastonbudget Music Fest, Wistow Music in the Park, and a LOROS Antiques Roadshow. In recent years LOROS has invited athletic supporters abroad to undertake sponsored treks on the Inca Trail, to Nepal or the Great Wall of China; in England to stride the Three Peaks Challenge or Coast-to-Coast Walk; and in Leicestershire to ramble the Charnwood Forest 'Walk on the Wild Side' or the Leicester city Twilight Walk. Perhaps the sheer demanding physicality of these walks arouses in its participants a soul-searching comparison with the frailty of the end-of-life experience.

In 2005 LOROS running costs amounted to £5 million, but this was of course covering an even more comprehensive palliative care service. In 2010 £7 million was required, but 90p in every £1 donated went direct to patient care. During the early years LOROS had received 75%-80% of its income from statutory funding, but in

A charity wheelbarrow race at Great Glen

2011 it receives only one-third. The Fundraising Team consists of ten salaried staff and five volunteers. There now remains only seven Support Groups in towns and villages, but high-profile Patrons, Ambassadors and a partnership in its 2009/10 season with Leicester City Football Club, are all exciting new ways of highlighting the essence of the LOROS spirit. Although the huge task of LOROS funding has increasingly been carried out by professional staff, who implement sophisticated and high-level techniques, the roots of the LOROS fundraising endeavour remain very much in the hearts, minds, energies and creativity of the people of Leicestershire and Rutland. Highly aware of this, the Team turns out at any time of day or evening, weekdays or weekends, to attend cheque presentation ceremonies, when they offer heartfelt thanks, and spread the word still further. The contagious LOROS bug has now become an epidemic – because anyone (including you) can do it!

Steve Walsh opening the new LOROS 4 Men shop in Wigston in 2011

CHAPTER NINE
ROYAL AND VIP VISITS
A Picture Gallery

Prince Charles and Princess Diana open the LOROS Hospice, 1986

Duchess of Gloucester opens the Hospice extension, 2000

LOROS presentation with Rugby player Martin Johnson

Duchess of Kent opens Manor Croft Extension, 1990

England Rugby players Dorian West & Julian White with the World Cup at the Hospice in 2003

Naturalist David Bellamy supports the LOROS Bird Box Campaign along with presenter Colin Green MBE

Model Melinda Messenger with LOROS patient Janet at the Ritz

Rugby's Rory Underwood at the Auction of Promises

Fitness guru Rosemary Conley with a LOROS patient

Broadcaster Martin Lewis opens the LOROS library

Media Star Cynthia Payne, speaker at a Ladies Luncheon

Tigers Rugby player Will Johnson with Matron Bronwen

Duchess of Gloucester opens Willow Wing 2010

Earl Spencer, speaker at a Ladies Luncheon, with Lady Gretton

Formula 1 racing driver Lewis Hamilton meeting a patient & family

Dave Bartram from Showaddywaddy & Alan Birchenall from L. C. F. C. at Great Glen Wheelbarrow Race

Leicester City Football Club visiting LOROS in 2010

Ann Widdecombe at LOROS Ladies Luncheon in 2011

Sven-Goran Eriksson, Diane Morris and Alan Birchenall at The Star Inn, Thrussington (courtesy of Lionel Heap)

LOROS Patrons Alan Birchenall and Mark Selby in 2010

Aspirations for the Future
by the Board of Trustees

LOROS has undoubtedly developed into a successful and well-known charity since its formation in 1977, with a positive reputation and marvellous support from the local community. However there are sometimes misconceptions about hospice care and the work of LOROS. For LOROS is still thought by some to be the place where older people with cancer go to die, or as a place only for people from one sector of our community.

The facts are rather different: cancer can affect people of any age and a fair number of those admitted to LOROS are in their twenties and thirties; many LOROS patients have conditions other than cancer, for example motor neurone disease, heart failure or kidney failure; around half of those who are admitted to the hospice inpatient unit go home again, either because they came in just for respite care or to enable their pain or other symptoms to be managed more effectively. LOROS also provides a wide range of care in the community and in people's homes, as well as different types of outpatient clinics. And most important of all, an individual becomes a LOROS patient because of medical need, independent of gender, race, colour, faith or the ability to pay. LOROS is working to enhance the awareness and understanding of its purpose to bridge these gaps between perception and reality. This remains a real challenge because the local community is geographically and culturally diverse; and many people are still reticent about engaging with the subject of death and dying.

The shape of our society will change over the coming decades with an ageing population, and there will be more people living longer with illness. The resultant demands on health and social care will be enormous. LOROS is well placed to respond to these challenges and has a number of wide-ranging aspirations for its future.

LOROS should be able to make an even greater contribution to integrated and genuinely 24 hour 7 day a week health services out in the community. LOROS will also strive to extend the provision of palliative care to a wider range of people with conditions other than cancer e.g. neurological conditions, based upon its experience and success in patients with motor neurone disease; whenever possible working with partners who have the relevant expertise. Along with other hospices and palliative care providers, LOROS will need to monitor and adapt its day care to meet the changing needs of patients who would benefit from such support. LOROS also needs to better engage with ethnic minority communities as well as hard-to-reach and disadvantaged groups, striving to be genuinely inclusive and available for the whole community of Leicester, Leicestershire and Rutland.

In addition to extending the impact and reach of direct patient care, LOROS will build on its already successful education programme for healthcare professionals, and also contribute more extensively to research which has the potential to improve palliative care.

LOROS will need in the future to foster an even stronger culture of innovation to both improve the quality of patient care and to make all it does as effective and efficient as possible. It must continue to attract and retain the best possible staff with the right skills and attitude of mind and provide them with a high quality working environment and a supportive culture where they feel valued and engaged with the overall aims of the organisation. LOROS must also continue to offer its remarkable group of volunteers a wide variety of fulfilling opportunities to support the charity, so that they feel their contribution is recognised and appreciated.

However, the scale of LOROS' ambition for the future needs to be realistic with plans which are financially sustainable. At the time of writing there is economic uncertainty in the UK, and the government's current drive to radically reform health and social care will undoubtedly have some impact on LOROS in the near future. Furthermore, the regulatory and legislative environment in which it operates is becoming increasingly onerous.

Whatever happens with government funding, the majority of financial support for LOROS will continue to come from the generous support of the local community. The financial assistance which LOROS receives from the community is very strong, and there continues to be a wide variety of ways in which people and organisations can support LOROS financially e.g. by making a donation; organising or attending a fundraising event; joining the lottery; donating to or buying items from one of its shops; and leaving a gift in a Will. LOROS will be working to increase awareness of the need for financial support through personal contact and a growing range of communication channels, including the burgeoning use of social networking tools, such as Facebook and Twitter.

There may be some future uncertainties, but there is confidence that the vision and ethos of LOROS will continue to flourish. When the next chapter of this book is written in perhaps ten years time, there is every reason to believe that LOROS will have realized its current aspirations and continued to develop, adapt and grow successfully, as it has done in the past. Above all, the focus and heart of LOROS has been and always will be the patients and their families.

APPENDIX (i)
Time Line

1975 Dec	Joint meeting of Leicester Council of Churches and Leicester Free Church Women's Council to secure better care for the terminally ill
1976 Jan	Hospice Project Group starts
1977 Mar	LOROS becomes a registered charity
1977 Nov	Inaugural public meeting at Leicester Town Hall
1980 Dec	Groby Road site is chosen for the Hospice
1981 Jan	LOROS first office opens at 18 Friar Lane, Leicester
1981 Mar	Fundraising Appeal is launched at University of Leicester
1984 Mar	The President, Lady Palmer, cuts the first turf at Groby Road site at start of work on Hospice building
1984 Apr	Manor Croft Day Centre receives its first patients
1984 June	First client is referred to Counselling service, based at Manor Croft
1985 Sept	First patient is admitted to the Hospice (registered for 12 beds only)
1985 Oct	Counselling Service moves to Hospice
1986 Feb	Hospice is licensed for 25 beds
1986 May	Prince and Princess of Wales officially open the Hospice
1989 Aug	First LOROS shop opens
1989 Jan	Manor Croft extension is completed
1990 July	The Duchess of Kent officially opens Manor Croft extension
1996 July	LOROS Lottery is launched
1997 Feb	Keith Vaz, M.P., officially opens the new Relatives' Suite
2000 May	The Duchess of Gloucester officially opens the Hospice extension
2004 Apr	5 new single-patient rooms are opened on the 'back corridor'; now 31 beds
2010 Mar	The Duchess of Gloucester officially opens the new Willow Wing

APPENDIX (ii)
Officers, Patrons and Ambassadors

President
1980-1983   The Right Revered Richard Rutt, Bishop of Leicester
1984-1995   Lady Palmer
1996-1999   Janet Atkins
2000-2011   Jennifer, Lady Gretton

Chairman of Trustees
1977-1984   Dr Andrew Cull
1985-1988   Barbara Keene
1989-1997   Kenneth Wood
1998-2003   Chris Hilton
2003-2009   Stephen Thomas
2010-2011   Prof. John Feehally

Bursar/Treasurer
1977-1981   Philip Hall
1982-1986   Jon Noakes
1987-1988   John Mynard
1989-2011   Andrew Stant

Administrator/Bursar/General Manager/Chief Executive
1981-1987   Anne Kind (Administrator; 1984 Public Liaison Officer)
1985-1988   Robert Alderton (Bursar)
1989-2008   Michael Archer (General Manager/Chief Executive)
2008-2011   Simon Proffitt (Chief Executive)

Medical Director/Lead Consultant
1985-1994   Dr Sam Ahmedzai
1995-1996   Dr Ian Johnson
1997-1998   Dr Gillian Rathbone
1999-2004   Dr Nicky Rudd
2005-2006   Dr Esther Waterhouse
2007-2011   Dr Luke Feathers

Matron/Director of Care Services
1985-2001   Bronwen Biswas
2001-2011   Chris Faulkner
2011   Joanne Kavanagh

Current Patrons
Alan Birchenall MBE
Martin Johnson CBE
Ali Mauchlen
Mark Selby

Current Ambassadors
Amarjit 'Tony' Bhaur
Derick Horsfall
Kay Johnson
Peter Jones
Kishor Mistry
Liz Seaston
Charlotte Thompson
Monica Winfield

Many other people have been Officers of LOROS and have given valuable service to the charity, but these are too numerous to mention by name.

APPENDIX (iii)
Biographies *alphabetically listed*

CHAPTER I, EARLY BEGINNINGS

The significant founding members of LOROS were:

Dr Anthony (Tony) Carr, a Leicester Clinical Pyscholgist, attended the very first meeting between LFCWC and LCC in December 1975. With Dr Cull, he drew up a Draft Research Proposal (1976) on the needs of the terminally ill. Appointed to the Steering Committee (1976), he was one of 'the terrible trio'. He co-produced The Rugg and Carr Report (1976)

Dr Andrew Cull, a General Practitioner, based at Uppingham Road Health Centre, Leicester, had a particular interest in hospice care. He was invited to attend the first Project Meeting (1976), was appointed to the Steering Committee and unanimously elected as its Chairman. Dr Cull emerged as a leader with intense drive and dedication and saw the goal of establishing a hospice in Leicester as all important. He was a man of great charisma and recruited many knowledgeable people with special expertise. His deep concern for LOROS sometimes led to differences of opinion and tensions, but these were mostly resolved. When he was not busy as a G.P., he was thinking, planning and scheming for LOROS. He worked ceaselessly for LOROS for nine years. His energy and determination to bring about the project's aspirations were enormous. But once the first patient had been admitted to the new Hospice, Dr Cull resigned his position as Chairman, to commence a new life away from Leicester.

Mr Philip Hall was appointed Treasurer at the first meeting of the new Council of Management (1977) and resigned the position in 1982, owing to ill health. Mr Hall and his wife, Marie, put an enormous amount of effort into LOROS in the early period, and Mrs Hall continued as a LOROS volunteer for many more years.

Mr John Hilton was appointed Director of Development for LOROS (1983), executing the plans and policies of the Council of Management, co-ordinating the activities of the Council and its Sub-Committees, the development of the Appeal and the co-ordination of fundraising activities. When he retired in 1985 Mr Hilton was elected a Vice-President, for he had been instrumental in raising £300,000 and had contributed to the professionalism of the organisation.

Mrs Anne Kind O.B.E. was running the Leicester Family Planning Clinic when in 1980 she was invited to become Adminstrator for LOROS. She accepted and in 1981 started working part-time in the tiny office at Friar Lane, becoming full-time and the first and only salaried member of staff a few months later. She inspired the general public, who flocked to the office with offers of financial help and would receive gifts of a few pence to many hundreds of pounds with the same delight and graciousness. She inaugurated a scheme for help from volunteers throughout Leicestershire and encouraged the countywide formation of LOROS Groups that within two years numbered sixty-four. Mrs Kind was also on the Speakers' Panel, giving talks throughout the county, and was particularly interested in school projects for LOROS. In 1984 her title was changed to Public Liaison Officer, to avoid confusion with that of Adminstrator of the Hospice. After her retirement in 1987 she was made a Vice-President, and in 1990 was awarded the O.B.E. for her work in the community. Her husband, Dr Bill Kind, became Chairman of the Counselling Service Committee, and of Manor Croft, where he acted as handy-man, plumber and carpenter. After his death in 1987 a plaque to him was unveiled at Manor Croft in grateful memory of his dedicated work there.

Mrs Barbara Keene, Chairman, a member of the Leicestershire Community Health Council, was known to be interested in the local Hospice project. In 1983 she was appointed Chairman of the Day Unit Steering Committee, set up to find a suitable premises that in due course became Manor Croft. She became increasingly involved with LOROS. Her experience and ability to co-ordinate the efforts of committee members towards their common goal was a special talent and her influence and dedication contributed to LOROS becoming known throughout the county. In 1984 she chaired the Furnishing Committee set up to select the furniture, carpets, curtains and colour schemes for the Hospice, and on the resignation of Dr Cull, was appointed Chairman. (1985-1989).

Mr Michael Marvell administered Leicester Charity Organisation Society (LCOS) at 18 Friar Lane Leicester. But it was he who had in 1972 organised that very first public meeting at Leicester Royal Infirmary. He was elected onto the first LOROS Steering Committee (1976), and became one of 'the terrible trio'. Mr Marvell provided vital liaison between potential financial donors and LOROS. He enabled people with resources to see the importance of LOROS and charmed them. Dr Cull was the 'doer' and Mr Marvell the 'enabler'. They formed the main plank with Dr Carr being a tremendous supporter for both. The Rugg and Carr Report was reproduced at Friar Lane, with Mr Marvell working most of one weekend there, literally camping out overnight and being resusitated with refreshments at midnight.

Lady Palmer came from London to live in Leicestershire in 1957 and is the mother of four daughters. Through experience in her own family, she had a personal interest in the care of the terminally ill and their families. She was appointed President of LOROS in 1984 and was heavily involved in the original Appeal. She fulfilled many speaking engagements and attended hundreds of public events. Lady Palmer regularly visited the Hospice, and Manor Croft patients were frequent visitors for afternoon tea at her home. For many years she chaired the LOROS President's Appeal Committee that regularly raised over £50,000 a year.

CHAPTER 3 IN-PATIENT CARE

The original 1985 Hospice triumvirate management team was:

Dr Sam Ahmedzai, Medical Director, a fully accredited Consultant, had been a Senior Registrar specialising in chest diseases at Glasgow Royal Infirmary and was involved with cancer medicine. He was founder of a Glasgow-based group for professional people working with the terminally ill. Dr Sam worked tirelessly to put LOROS on the map, both nationally and internationally. On leaving LOROS he took up the prestigious post of Professor of Palliative Medicine and Director of the Trent Palliative Care Centre in Sheffield. Matron Bronwen's memories of him include his passion for pens and exotic plants, and his belief in the benefits to patients of all kinds of animals. She described him as an exciting, stimulating, challenging and demanding colleague, who seemed to possess limitless amounts of energy and had a terrific sense of humour.

Robert Alderton, Bursar, formerly Chief Administrator of the South Derbyshire Health Authority, was Chairman of the LOROS Management Team. He is remembered for his kindness and enthusiasm, and for guiding people in a calm and encouraging manner. When he retired he was appointed a LOROS Vice-President.

Bronwen Biswas, Matron, qualified as an SRN at Leeds Royal Infirmary in 1964 and spent eight years working in Canada. She came to Leicester as a student Health Visitor in 1972 and in due course became Assistant Director of Health Visiting. At LOROS she approached her work in a calm, professional manner, with the utmost care and sincerity, and the patients and staff loved her. On retiring in 2001 it was recorded that 'she showed a determined dedication to the patients and their families, commitment to her staff, to LOROS, and to the wider hospice movement. In Bronwen her staff knew they had a champion and a manager who was fair and firm. In LOROS's name she attended galas, concerts, pubs, clubs, spoke on the radio and welcomed TV camera crews. She helped to build the reputation of the Hospice, both locally and nationally, being a voice for Palliative Care at National Level.

APPENDIX (iv)
LOROS Services and Aims

LOROS, the Leicestershire & Rutland Hospice, is a charity whose aim is to enhance the quality of life of patients with cancer and some other life limiting illnesses for whom curative treatment is no longer possible, together with support for the family. LOROS also contributes to the education and training of healthcare professionals and has a commitment to research in palliative care.

LOROS is a local charity run by local people for the benefit of local patients and their families. Over 2,500 patients access our services each year

LOROS services include:-
- In-patient unit of 31 beds
- Medical Outpatient Clinics
- Palliative Day Therapy Unit
- Complementary Therapy Clinics
- Counselling for patients and their families
- Community Nurse Specialist Team
- Lymphoedema Clinics
- Family Support Service
- Chaplaincy
- Cultural Support Worker
- Enablement (Physiotherapy, Occupational Therapy and Social Worker)

All of these services are provided free to patients and their families.

LOROS itself needs to raise in excess of £4 million (in 2011) annually to fund these services and to provide development. The Charity relies on the support of the local community in order to raise these vital funds.

LOROS

Leicestershire & Rutland Hospice, Groby Road, Leicester LE3 9QE
Tel. 0116 231 3771

LOROS Manor Croft. Palliative Day Therapy Unit, Manor Croft, 147 Ratcliffe Road, Leicester LE2 3TE Tel. 0116 270 7330

LOROS Shops/Lottery. Enterprise House, 1 Station Road, Glenfield, LE3 8BT Tel. 0116 231 3666

LOROS Fundraising. Tel 0116 231 8431/2

Registered Charity No. 506120. Registered in England and Wales 1298456

Bibliography and Acknowledgements

Clitheroe, Dr Edna (1991), *Birth of a Hospice: history of the Leicestershire Organisation for the Relief of Suffering (LOROS), the First Years, 1975-1986*

Taylor, Wendy (2010) *Silver Linings*

LOROS newsletters 1978-2011

Leicester Mercury *Photographs and articles*

THANK YOU to the many people connected with LOROS whom I have interviewed; to those who have read and commented on my draft text and assisted with illustrations; to the publishing team; and to my husband and family who have supported and encouraged me throughout. C.W.

ABOUT THE AUTHOR

CAROLINE WESSEL was born and bred in Leicestershire. She is a former trustee of LOROS, is currently Chairman of the Leicestershire & Rutland County Nursing Association, and a trustee of a number of other local charities. She has a M.A. in Victorian Studies from the University of Leicester and has published extensively on historical topics. Titles include *The Knights Hospitaller of St John in Leicestershire*, *High Sheriffs in Leicestershire* and *A Portrait of Beaumanor*. Caroline serves on the committee of the Leicestershire Archaeological & Historical Society and is President of the Desford & District Local History Society.

Copyright © 2011 C.M.Wessel